The True Nature Of Human Nature
The Symbiotic Parasite Known as Religion

Independently published

www.thetruenatureofhumannature.com

February 2019 printing

Unless otherwise indicated, Scripture quotations are from the New International Version®, NIV® Copyright ©1973, 1978, 1984, 2011, published by Biblica, Inc.®

Trademarks: All trademarks are the property of their respective owners. The publisher is not associated with any product or vendor mentioned in this book.

Cover Artwork by Orlando Rodriguez
Book Design by Orlando Rodriguez
Edited by Elke Lopez

The True Nature Of Human Nature

ISBN: 978-1-7909878-8-7

The True Nature Of Human Nature
The Symbiotic Parasite Known as Religion

Orlando Rodriguez

An excuse is worse and more terrible than a lie,
for an excuse is a lie guarded.
— Pope John Paul II

It's not a lie if you believe it.
— George Costanza

To my son Preston
who would not be alive
if not for his loving Mommy

Contents

Acknowledgements

I can't believe I am writing this portion of my book. This means it is finally done! To my loving wife, Elke. I am thankful for all the support you have given me during this most arduous of times. Writing a complete book has been the most difficult thing I have ever done, and you have always been there as a source of encouragement when I needed it the most. Every time I wanted to give up, you were able to put me back on track. Thank you for every edit, re-edit and comment you have given, showing me things I was blinded to due to writing for such a long time. To my wonderful children. Thank you for putting up with two and a half years of daddy's writing. I know this came between us and playtime, but I promise to play some Fortnite and spend quality time with each of you. A special thanks to Christine Hayes from Yale University for helping put out the 24-video compilation of Open Yale Courses, Introduction to the Old Testament. It changed my whole way of thinking about the Bible, and for that, I am forever grateful.

Prologue

Every word put to paper was purposefully done. Every sentence was intentionally crafted. There may be a smattering of passion in the course of this work, but the result of this undertaking was calculated. What was my purpose in writing this book? Is this a writing of passion or anger? Contempt or concealed contrition? What was my motive?

I was born into the religion of Jehovah's Witnesses and was raised by my forebears with the single-minded goal to be baptized in the name of the Lord, Jehovah. Lucky me. There was a problem with this monomaniacal plan. I was an atheist as far back as I could remember.

Before I continue, I'd like to make the following requisite statement which I think is very important to articulate. I promised myself that I did not want to make another Jehovah Witness bashing book. There are plenty of those available that convey the intentional internal conflict that is nourished in the congregation and the ideologies used as brainwashing you to accept the "truth." However, I think some background is required to understand the vector of my thoughts and how I ended up on my laptop, typing away ferociously on the topic of religion.

As mentioned previously, I was an atheist as far back as I could remember. I was always interested in science. It seemed to be the only thing that could quench the innate thirst of my mind. Very quickly, I started to realize that religion and reality could not coexist and that lies were being told.

My first encounter was with dinosaurs when I was about eight years of age. I would ask, "Why would Jehovah create dinosaurs, just to kill them later?". It didn't seem moral to me that these creatures were not given a chance to survive. The answer that I received was *"Jehovah had his reason for creating dinosaurs, and once his will was accomplished, they were no longer needed. All we can understand is that there was a purpose to these dinosaurs and that their removal from this world occurred after their purpose was fulfilled*". That concept seemed quite difficult to comprehend. If we were created by the Lord, like the dinosaurs, it would not matter if a mystical book described our future destiny. The bible could be a lie; we could fulfill our "purpose" in the mind of God and be next on the extermination list! It also shows that murder was prevalent before the sin of Adam and Eve. If moral perception is somewhat logical, then it should be distributed evenly, regardless of our biases.

Things became progressively worse. Now being fully entombed in the study of science, studying physics, astronomy, and cosmology, I came to the theory of the Big Bang, with the discovered cosmic microwave background radiation (CMB) providing corroborative evidence to this theory which was in direct contrast to the indoctrinated idea of creation. Did God create the Big Bang? Jehovah's Witnesses do not ascribe to this mode of thinking, regularly invoking the scripture that *"God is not a God of disorder but of peace - as in all the congregations of the Lord's people."* – 1 Corinthians 14:33. Because of this scripture and others, they will hold hard onto the ideology promulgated by the creation story in the book of Genesis that states that God created all things personally.

Afterward, the study of evolution was the next point of contention. What I learned was disheartening, due to my forced faith. If God created all animals and the first humans at the Garden of Eden then why are there fossils of animals of prehistoric origins found throughout the entire world? One can argue that God created animals throughout the world at different times, but the Bible clearly states that man, the first man was placed in the Garden of Eden. This is delineated as the starting point for humanity. Therefore, we should find the first human fossils in this area or the surrounding areas. This is not the case. We find the first early human fossils in Africa, not in the area we now call the *"fertile crescent."* The fossilized evidence clearly circumscribes the epicenter of origin for humans in Africa, in clear contradiction with the bible creation story. It essentially negates the Garden of Eden concept, unless you interpret that scripture as a parable. It is this reason why many people do. More on this evasion of doctrinal responsibility later.

I also questioned the makeup of ourselves. If God created us, why is our physiology extensions of other animals? If you look at the bone structures of all vertebrates, they are all essentially the same! The human, the dog, the bird, and the whale all have the same arm bone structure. Yes, we look very different on the outside but look inside, see our skeletons and realize that we all have fingers, wrists, and joints, all relatively placed in the same manner as other vertebrates. We all predominantly have eyeballs, teeth, and noses. Even fish have noses! These are all shared commonalities in all vertebrates. What does that say? Is this blueprint for life perfect? Far from it. It shows that we all essentially came from the same predecessor; that we are all animals and are related. The scientific evidence for evolution is overwhelming. The theory of evolution and the Bible do not align with each other. In a fundamentalist household, fact remained in the aisle of science and would never trespass onto scripture. If there was a contradiction between the two disciplines, I was told that the Bible was the authority and should be upheld, regardless of what some "worldly" scientist may state. Without going into further detail, I could say I was thoroughly confused.

The problem with my childhood indoctrination was that, as you will come to realize in the book, religion is a parasite and you are going to run into some issues when you try to escape from its possession, whether you like it or not. Once you are infected, it stays with you for life. Religion is quite similar to alcoholism or any illicit drug dependence. The best form of treatment is to abstain.

After some time had passed, with much toiling and churning, I was baptized at the age of 17. I remember that I proceeded forward with the ritual of baptism not because I believed in God, but because I wanted to be accepted among the young group of Jehovah's Witnesses. It was really "the thing to do"! It was comparable to a sweet sixteen for a woman or turning 21 and having your first legal drink. It was a coming of age moment, and yet that in itself is not philosophically honest. If you passed a certain age (this applies only to those being born into the faith) and you were not baptized, parishioners suspected there was either something wrong with you or that you were bad association.

After baptism, I became quite religious, studying the bible intensively, trying to reconcile my concrete foundation of scientific knowledge with my faith. I became an introverted apologist. I tried to quiet the logical screaming in my mind with bible based principles!

At 18 I realized this path of life was ridiculous! Nothing made sense. No amount of faith-based gymnastics could subsume all of the terrestrially discovered and acquired evidence into the biblical text. No matter how many scriptures the elders (pastors of the Jehovah's Witness religion) threw at me; "the earth hangs upon nothing" or "circle of the earth", it truly made no sense and my sticking point in this tribunal of my consciousness was the 1st and 2nd chapter of the book of Genesis. I go into detail about my objections in this book. All that was offered to me as an explanation to my queries were Watchtower articles that attempted to reconcile the Bible with science and constant inquiries as to whether or not I still believed in God.

I felt the armor of my calloused faith chipping away with each intellectual blow, freeing myself from the petty attachments of doctrine. The issue however with the parasite of religion is that it is similar to the AIDS virus and many other virulent strains. Once you catch it, it stays with you forever. You may be able to sever the connection of this sinister symbiotic relationship, but it is always lurking in the back of the mind, once you have been exposed to this mental empathogen.

Prologue

I stopped going to "church," met my wife and dated only five months before getting married. We were married in a civil ceremony because our families (my wife was raised as a Jehovah's Witness as well; the irony) would not attend a "worldly" wedding.

My wife and I were married, and everything was fantastic until the birth of my first biological son Cristian, aptly named. My "stepson" Taylor is from a previous marriage, although I would never dream of using the prefix "step" in my home. He was my "first son." Regardless, something peculiar occurred. I felt compelled to go back to the organization of Jehovah's Witnesses. I still realized in the privacy of my mind that everything that was wrong with this faith was still active, but the "devil's advocate" housed in the frontal lobe of my cerebrum asked me, *what is a better gift to give your child than everlasting life?* I wanted to give my child the best there was to offer in life, knowing full and well that this religion was not going to accomplish my directive. Nonetheless, something in my mind compelled me to continue in this direction.

A week after my son was born, we migrated to a Kingdom Hall located in Astoria, Queens for the annual commemoration of Jesus' death called "The Memorial." This is the most sacred event you could attend in the Jehovah's Witness faith. We were one of the last ones to arrive, and it was packed. We were literally touching the back door. We remained standing for an hour as they went through the procession of the event and listened to the discourse.

My wife was up in arms over the sudden change in belief and my compulsion to revert into a wholly religious person. I again told her that I wanted to give our children the gift of everlasting life. She was so perplexed with my abnormally capricious behavior, and she fought me on the matter till the very end. Unfortunately, I won the argument.

We went back. We went back to the "truth." Afterward, many things happened. Some of the things that occurred I choose not to explain in this book for the sake of being terse and succinct.

Prologue

The main point of religious contention however that allowed me to pivot out of the "Witness Organization" was the situation that occurred with the birth of my second biological son (3rd son), Preston.

Preston was going to be born with a rare heart condition known as "Transposition of the Great Arteries," also known as TGA. Without going into the finer details, the layman explanation of the condition is that the heart was fine, but the arteries, the plumbing of the heart, was inversely installed. The oxygenated blood that was meant for the body was re-pumped back to the lungs, and the deoxygenated blood destined to be replenished with oxygen in the lungs was redistributed into the body again. In essence, he was going to choke to death almost as soon as he left the safety of the womb. He would die in minutes, hours or days. If there were sufficient mixing in the heart (something that occurs in almost all newborns), he would live a month or two tops. The diagnosis of TGA was a death sentence. A baby born with TGA, if no remedial is done, will die. It is certain death.

Herein lies the issue. The Jehovah's Witness organization does not allow the use of blood transfusions. They use the bible as evidence that God would not allow such a thing. If a Witness were to proceed with a transfusion, they would be disfellowshipped, the most severe form of excommunication that exists.

Here is the defining moment for me personally. My wife followed her own path to emancipation, and I am happy to say we all met at the same destination of peace. We found the best doctor in the world to do the procedure, Dr. Jan Quaegebeur and the procedure in his hands had a 99% success rate. We discussed with the other doctors that we needed this to be a bloodless surgery, and they agreed to do their best. They gave our son blood expanders and would recycle his blood as required.

However, the day of the surgery came and Dr. Q, as he is called at the hospital came up to us and said that he would do the best to

Prologue

avoid a blood transfusion but that he could not guarantee a bloodless surgery. There is a certain amount of blood required in the blood pump before it can operate and being that Preston was two weeks old, he did not have a lot of blood available. I kept saying out loud *"this is supposed to be a bloodless surgery!"* but my loving wife intervened and said, *"Please do whatever it takes to save our son"* and she signed the requisite waivers. I felt relieved that my wife made the tough decision but also ashamed. Did this false religion mean more to me than my son? See chapter 4 for a more in-depth view of this situation under the discussion of "Social Compliance." I feel that in the end, I would have caved in and accepted the procedure with blood, but I will never truly know. I only know that I have Dr. Q and my loving, intelligent wife to thank in saving the life of my son. A blood transfusion was, in fact, necessary or the chance for death was certain. I never wanted to broach the subject again, but my wife did and one day asked *"Are you ok with my decision for a blood transfusion? I pick the life of my son over God".* I agreed with her decision, with the weight of my shame in full view of my facial features. I thanked her for doing what I was not ready to do, save our son over God.

The damage was done, however. There was a point where I may have allowed my son to die for the cause of religion. This was tantamount to a mother of a radicalized Muslim being happy that her child was martyred for an Islamic cause. I will carry this burden of disgust for the rest of my life. I hope Preston will forgive me when he is older and hears this part of his story for the first time.

The surgery was a success! He healed wonderfully and is now a rambunctious 6-year-old. In addition to the second chance my son was given, I was given a second chance in life as well. I felt the connection with the parasite of religion sever. Unfortunately, I continued to attend the Kingdom Hall, not out of belief in God but out of necessity. My friends and family were there, and the roots that I grew in the new neighborhood we moved to was entrenched with the religion. I was invested in the "truth." As you will see, although you may have severed the connection of the parasite, you are still infected, and it cannot die. It can merely go into remission. Then the following happened.

I remember the day clearly. I was sitting in the Kingdom Hall during the study of the Watchtower; the magazine Witnesses hawk to people during their required door to door preaching. The Elder asked a question to a particular paragraph. There are predetermined questions to paragraphs that are created by the organization to force feed doctrine. There is no thought given to the question. You literally can read the answer from the paragraph.

A young brother (a male Jehovah's Witness), who was a friend of my son Taylor, who will remain nameless, raised his hand to answer. I didn't prepare for the study, so I had no idea what was about to occur.

The question was in essence "What should you do or think if you come across a scripture that troubles you?" The answer from this young man struck the very fiber of my being.

"If you don't understand a scripture or find it troubling, maybe the issue is not with the scripture. Maybe the problem is with you! We need to know that God is a loving God and even if we feel that he was too harsh in a scripture, he was just. Also, as we have learned in previous studies, we should avoid individual thinking. Individual thinking is dangerous! We need to remain steadfast to Jehovah and his word" this young man answered.

I was horrified. All of the study I put forth to science was worthless because I should not think individually as a person? I knew that this was part of being a Jehovah's Witness all along but having it said for all to hear was unbearable. Did I want my children to be raised in the brackish stench of this environment, their mental faculties removed and replaced with autonomous robotic programming? Did I want to raise non-thinking drones?

Prologue

I remember thinking "What the hell?" My wife turned to me. With eyes wide open I realized that I was dictating my thoughts out loud! I stood up and went for a walk in the parking lot, pacing back and forth, pondering on why I was still here, after the near-death experience directly created by the religion and its people.

I decided to refuse to be part of this militaristic theology. The Jehovah's Witnesses request to quash individual thinking was an attempt to delegitimize my voice and the voice of others. After that, my family and I quickly degenerated from the "truth."

So, why am I writing the book? I realize that I did not write this book out of passion, anger, contempt or hidden contrition. I wrote the book because through experiences I realized that there are many ways to reach people infected with the religion parasite, but in many instances, the blunt force trauma of knowledge was the only way to truly sever the symbiotic connection. The connection will always be there but the more you damage it, the harder it is for the parasite to resurface.

If we truly want to liberate our minds from the teachings of mythology purported in the guise of the omniscient God, serious damage needs to be done to this parasite to release ourselves from this epistemological bullshit. Now, some of the phrasing in this book may be harsh. It is intended to be this way so that maximum damage can be inflicted upon this illness and so that true abandonment of this religious garbage can be achieved.

I am thankful for the Atheists and Agnostics who purchase this book because it may provide some additional ammunition in the war between religion and reality. I am, however, more thankful for the Deists and Theists who purchase this book, in hopes that this writing may dissolve the chains of mental shackles that have been imposed upon them by this hateful illness. There is no salvation in God, regardless what the person at the platform or pulpit may say. There is no future, except for the one you are currently facing. Please hold on with both hands as you embark on

Prologue

the journey called life because not only is it a bumpy ride, it's the only ride you have. Please enjoy every emotion and experience that you have, regardless if it is good or bad. In the end, those feelings are yours and yours only. There is no God.

Introduction

I have found that a person can never truly know their position on a matter, whether it be social, political, economic or ethical until they have written a book or large paper on the subject. This written work should be void of any language embellishments, be stripped down to its epistemological roots and should be somewhat scholarly, with peer-reviewed sources included where possible. The reason I say this is because until you put the words down on paper and start to make some semblance of what is in the privacy of your mind, you are not truly aware of all the aspects of the position itself. When you write out your stance, you are faced with creating a cohesive and continuous position regardless of the paths that it may take you. You do not truly understand a particular topic if you cannot speak of it in the language of irreducible complexity, which I will try to do. What I am about to do is to provide in some respects an introspective understanding of the position I hold. Let's see where this goes.

Chapter One

If the apocalypse comes, beep me.
- Buffy the Vampire Slayer

What is the first thing that comes to your mind when you first wake up? "Hit the snooze button?" or perhaps it may be "What's the weather like" when you look out the window? If you are one of the millions that have standard working hours in first or second world countries, then this may be an accurate description of your waking moments. However, if you are one of the many who resides in one of the war-torn areas of the world, your first thought, ascending into consciousness may be "I'm still alive!" or "Thank God for another day!" How sad is it that the circumference of hostility for many is so vast and yet, so mobile! How did humanity incur this hefty price of destructiveness? Many think that it is the inevitable consequence of living with others. Others see capitalism and other forms of economic faculties are to blame. There are others, however, that view this as the imminent conclusion depicted in the holy writings of the main tomes of the Judeo-Christian deities. What is the correct answer? Does it matter? If

The Religious Reality

one believes in something that is true or not, does it influence the outcome in any way? If so, is the influence measurable?

In order to emancipate our thoughts from beliefs moving forward, we need to reference the quantifiable exclusively, so there are a few things that need to be discussed before we depart on our guided thought experiment. There are very few original ideas in this book. There are very few original thoughts in general available to the extant populace due to the amount of time the information age has been operating. However, my goal is to accrete these ideas into one general use pill for everyone's inoculation. This world needs it. Regardless of the pushback I may receive from this publication; I find it my fiduciary duty to humanity to discharge these arcane falsehoods and myths so that human beings, the great apes of this populace (said with no malice), can come to educated conclusions. No longer should Homo sapiens be yoked to such superstitious tomfoolery. We all need to understand the origins of religion, why was religion necessary during humanities infancy, what purpose did it fulfill, is it still necessary but more importantly, is it true? I'm going to spoil the ending of this book and tell you that God, whether in the Judeo-Christian, Islamic, Hindu or other archaic format does not exist. It is a fundamental lie that is being taught to many at an early age, a form of Spartan child rearing, an austere way of living and should be viewed as a major form of child abuse, which has been a view from some educators for some time. Christianization has shown us through example that it was either feast or famine during the Dark Ages and Classical Antiquity. The pantheon of Catholicism and its deviant lords sought out the deserving, by force and disposed of the perceived spiritually defective, thus bringing rise to more apocalyptic beasts, namely Islam. But this should insult no one. Let us remember that it was the prophecies of Judaism that formed the basic tenants of Christianity. Cats do not breed dogs. They breed more of their same kind. In this same reasoning, monsters give birth to more monsters.

If anyone feels insulted by the previous statements, rest assured that this was not my intention. My only intention is to elicit an emotional response from those who have crystallized their beliefs and feel that debate on this most important of matters is irrelevant. Their faith should be tested since that is the basic theorem of scientific study, but for those with spiritual slants, please reference Hebrews 11:17-18. It states that *"By faith Abraham when God tested him, offered Isaac as a sacrifice. He who had embraced the promises was about to sacrifice his one and only son, even though God had said to him, "It is through Isaac that your offspring will be reckoned."* I want to pull apart the false veneer of apostasy and show that healthy and educated debate can reap positive results that have grand implications for future generations and oneself. Let us not forget that as a species, we are selfish and we seek things for our own initiative. These debates need to either bring options or closure, depending on your unique situation. The problem with religion, or more precisely, one of the main issues with religion is that one is punished for seeking the truth, although they are purportedly selling the truth wholesale for all those who seek it. See the hypocrisy there? They teach the truth but will steer you away from testing your faith. This is tantamount to an elementary teacher teaching basic arithmetic but indicating to the class not to research math in general because there will be others that state that math is false. The hubris of that statement is profound. It reverberates with the original rationalization from leading Christian followers during the "Dark Ages" that the Bible was off limits to commoners. Let's forgo the obvious fact that the majority of the population was illiterate and would not have been able to read an actual Bible. It is a fact that the Bible was fully accessible to a fortunate few. This was done with prejudice, not out of consequence.

Think for a moment. What purpose does religion provide? Does it provide us hope? Peace? A reason for existence, a purpose? Well, as we delve into the matter, later on, the purpose was for understanding, the same function of philosophy and science. So, why are my attacks on religion not homologous with the other disciplines above? Although I am not a fan of philosophy, for all intents and purposes there is logical reasoning behind its design. Science, however, works on a distinctive plane of understanding. Science determines not only to prove something to be true but also to disprove it. This is done through many cautious yet rational pathways referred to as the "scientific method." The general premise of this method is the creation of a hypothesis, the evaluation of the hypothesis through experiment, controlled experimentation, peer review and other forms of quality control. Religion, on the other hand, works on an entirely different principal. Religion decides what is true in the first place and then looks for scientific facts or any facts in general, to prop up its astonishing claims. They automatically discount anything that contradicts with their holy writings but accept anything, regardless of how comical it may sound, that harmonizes with their "truth." This is directly counter to how science operates. Who are we to decide what method is correct? Let us use logic of course! The following two stories will outline the principals of each, and we can then declare what is fact and what is fiction.

Sir Isaac Newton's published work "Mathematical Principles of Natural Philosophy," known as Principia, was groundbreaking science during the end of the 17th century. It expressed the law of universal gravitation in a clear and concise formula that was easy to understand and passed all forms of experimentation, expounding on the fundamental ideas from his predecessors Nicolaus

5
The Religious Reality

Copernicus and Johannes Kepler. The law stated that any two bodies would attract to each other with a force that is directly proportional to the product of their masses and is inverse the square of the distance between the two bodies. This was easily confirmed observing the moons orbit and doing the calculations to predict the distance the moon traveled per second. This revolutionized how we looked at the solar system and in turn, space in general. How impactful was this theory? In 1781 the astronomer Anders Johan Lexell mapped the complete orbit of Uranus and noticed perturbations in its proposed orbit. A perturbation in an orbit is the deviation from the predicted path of travel; a prediction created using the law of gravitation. He declared that there might be a possible celestial body beyond Uranus that could be altering the calculated path with its gravitational field. This is an important paradigm shift, where scientific inquiry meets predictions propagated by classical mechanics and the mathematical equations derived from it. You see, Neptune, an unknown planet at the time is too faint to be seen with the naked eye. Therefore, with the physical and mental tools available at the time, it would be comparable to finding a very specific needle in an unusually large needle stack. It was not until the late 19th century that mathematician Urbain Jean Joseph Le Verrier, using the data collected by Lexell began to calculate the perturbations between the methodic variations observed in Uranus's orbit and the predicted trajectory calculated by Newton's law of gravitation. What happened next changed the course of science and in essence, human history. In 1846 Johann Gottfried Galle and Heinrich d'Arrest from the Berlin Observatory, using Le Verrier's calculations, discovered the obscure planet we now call Neptune and more importantly, they found it within 1° of the predicted location. This was a stunning affirmation of Newton's laws and the demonstrative capabilities of modern science and its astonishing potential to making precise predictions, unlike the charlatans of days past and today that claim to know when the world will end and how, only to fail time and time again.

Our next story starts at the beginning. Genesis 1:1 – *"In the beginning, God created the heavens and the earth."* God creates all forms of life, perfect, devoid of sin and places them in the Garden of Eden. Adam and Eve sin, is cast out of paradise and introduce sin into the world. Romans 6:23 states *"For the wages sin pays is death"* so through the Bible, since 2 Timothy 3:16 states that *"All scripture is inspired by God and beneficial for teaching, reproving and setting things straight,"* we can see that death only occurred after the original sin. Man and animals begin to die (supposedly dinosaurs existed with humans if you are a young earth creationist and they are not even acutely aware of the monsters that existed during the Carboniferous and Permian periods) and the world becomes wicked. God confuses the languages of the people on earth during the building of the tower of Babel and humanity proliferates the earth. There is a global flood that eliminates all living beings that no longer live in this modern era, as per Genesis 7:23 which states *"So he wiped every living thing from the surface of the earth."* Let's ignore the fact that there is robust plant life that is estimated to be at least 80,000 years old, explicitly referencing the Pando also known as The Trembling Giant, as proof that this myth is false. The waters recede and then after some time and an apparent request for human sacrifice (Genesis 22:2), God's chosen people are exiled from Egyptian slavery. God sends a member of humanity to save his people from the possession of the Egyptian King, and after ten plagues, the King relinquishes authority of God's people. God's exclusive club of homo sapiens now become the people of Israel. However, there is immense infighting, and soon, this new nation is divided into two. Fast forward past the nationalistic wars and bloodshed, which we will touch upon later,

The Religious Reality

past the birth and death of the Messiah and to our current time, and we have prediction after prediction from the rulers of sovereign religions fail to materialize, one after another without recompense for their continuous failures.

This desire for human understanding has transformed humanity's original requisites into a tale of two divergent paths, one actively looking for truth and the other accepting written "truth" as gospel, vigorously protecting it at every turn. It is this fundamental distinction that separates these two ideologies and precludes the two from ever converging. Science can make predictions, but religion can only make post-dictions, a form of hindsight bias. The issues that arise are two-fold, and it relates to the reasoning of each party. The members of the religious establishment fully accept their leader's declarations of truth and will spread these central, fundamental beliefs by either direct proselytization or through indirect condemnation. A person, and I specifically use Christianity in this example, who does not accept God as their Lord and Savior is considered worldly or labeled a fool. The fact that you were born into sin, through no fault of your own, and deny the deity that has created this universe with you in mind is asinine. They claim that the other party should be ashamed of themselves as they drown in their pool of stupidity. However, it is important to remember that none of this will be said to you directly, only inferred with their smirk of disapproval as they listen to you speak. This example does not take into account people who view themselves as Christian but are not overtly religious and cherry pick which portions of the holy tenants they will follow. These latter individuals are religious only because of their upbringing and fear of reproach by their practicing parents. These people are intellectually lazy, have no backbone and therefore have no place in any of my arguments. The scientifically literate population, on the other hand, does not seem to care whether or not you follow a

The Religious Reality

religious conformity applicable to your geographic location. Regardless, when they hear religious observers speak and state their beliefs but then follow up their claims with fallacious arguments and nonsensical drivel, they are compelled to repudiate their assertions as false. They feel that it is their moral responsibility to correct this individual and to show them what the facts conclude. They shudder at the fact that people in this day and age are still following the myth and superstition found in the current assemblage of holy texts and respond with facetious retorts, downplaying a believer's declarations.

This is, in essence, the fundamental reason why religion and science will never see eye to eye. Religion declares their beliefs to be true and will find any nugget of fact to support their position. Science states that truth can only be found through rigorous and thorough use of the scientific method. The scientific community also feels compunction for those that are convolved to their ill-found faith, for many noble reasons that we will discuss later, so there is no middle ground, no general arena where these two parties may coexist and mingle. This is however irrelevant, once you understand how reality works. The real world works on facts, tangible systems, and natural laws. Intercession of deities have no place in this world and faith can only fuel senseless debates but do nothing to your gas tank. Gospel hymns may cheer people up and warm their hearts but cannot compare to a hug from a loved one or friend. Proverbs may sound like they are full of understanding but have no currency in intelligent discussion. The pastor must remain confined at the podium as long as the scientist is allowed to work in their lab. If you are choking on food, do you want a stranger to perform the Heimlich maneuver or pray for you? If you are held at gunpoint in an alley, and a passerby sees you, do you want them to call the police or for them to be fully comfortable in the fact that God has a plan for every one of us? To

The Religious Reality

pay bills, do you create a budget or do you believe that the money just will be there? If your life is in someone else's hands, do you want that individual to cherish the one life you have and do everything possible to save it or should that person feel that whatever happens is ok because if you were good, you go to heaven? If your child needs open heart surgery, who do you want at your disposal, a surgeon for the operation or a priest for their eulogy?

I submit to you ladies and gentlemen that as a member of the second group, although I may seem harsh with many of the facts that I shall present and how they negatively implicate the religious establishment, I assert these statements with no malice. I gladly cite my bias as an individual that sees this planet being torn asunder and feels the need that although hopeless as it may be to educate the devout masses and as religious as it may sound, if I have in some way saved one soul, then I have done my job. Again, very few of the ideas presented in this book are original, but I feel that the current arguments have not been distributed properly to the disenfranchised members of the religious society. For example, we know that AIDS is a killer that must be stopped for certain areas of the population to recover, namely parts of Africa. However, according to Pope Benedict XVI, AIDS is "a tragedy that cannot be overcome by money alone, that cannot be overcome through the distribution of condoms, which even aggravates the problems", in essence claiming that condoms could make the African AIDS crisis worse, showing that this religious order is more interested in retaining its spiritual dogma than human safety. It will stop at nothing to propagate the vile moral instruction disclosed in the foul work of writings such as the Bible. If the science of STD dispersion was emphasized more and if these erroneous statements by the religious right were suppressed in the African population and greater provisions were given to

The Religious Reality

spread the use of condoms in Africa, I would postulate that the AIDS epidemic in this region would be tamed to some degree. We must give trust in facts, not myth and legend. When was the last time that the myth of a rain god was used by farmers? When did a rain dance ritual provide its intended outcome? Never. What are farmers to do in times of need? Well, they can turn to the weather channel to see when the next rain is expected. They can also use tested irrigation techniques to maximize groundwater reserves and take advantage of new data stored and software created to help manage water. It is obvious to even the most oblivious person that science helped this situation and that the myth of a mystic rain god did not. This is a real-life example as to how religion is damaging our global society. Let us not make excuses for God.

However, if religion is so damaging, why does it exist? If not by a creator, where did religion come from? Was it necessary and if so, why?

Chapter Two

It is not death that a man should fear,
but he should fear never beginning to live.
-Marcus Aurelius

The theory is that our wholehearted faith will lead us to the man himself. The one who knows. The one who cares. And this is how religion begins. The doubt. The fever. The thirst for understanding. The hunger pangs of distress. Hopelessness in a world that could only be characterized as a successor to Jurassic Park in the eyes of our earliest ancestors. The feeling of weakness. These faceless faces, their lips, quivering in petrification of the unknown when explanation escaped their bosoms. The fear. The need for purpose. They are trying to understand this life of chess without knowing the rules of the game. They were not aware of the size or shape of the chessboard. They were not even aware that life was a game, a game of survival. Picture an avatar inserted into the competition of life, without being told the goal. Imagine Katniss Everdeen being dropped onto the forest without being told that she is a part of the Hunger Games. The title to this real-life enigmatic game? Darwinian Evolution. Without a manual for

Fear Brings About Religion

understanding, once they became truly sentient, this world must have been terrifying. It must have felt like divine providence when God was unveiled to all the players in one form or another. As our ancient progenitors grappled with the idea of a thing, an entity more superior to themselves, they started to create myths. Life's reality in many cases does not match with our perceptions. We fight against the harmonic dissonance of reality by generating stories.

These stories strived to explain everything surrounding them. Where do plants come from? Other plants. How? Seeds. Where do the seeds come from? God. Seeds alone create plants? They need water. Where does water come from? The sky. Why? So that we can drink and so that plants can drink. How? It was via a rain god. In what way? A rain dance. Question. What will happen to life without water once we have made a god unhappy? Will it stop raining if you stop dancing? What becomes of life once the shutters of the heavens are closed, holding back its voluminous contents? Why such discordance between fiction and reality? Why attach these blanket statements of certainty when they cannot apply to real life factual claims? Why do we create myths to decipher these environmental conditions?

That position as mentioned above sounds quite unhinged, one that no one in his or her right mind would hold today but this was not today. This was yesterday, magnified by 20,000 to 30,000 years and possibly much further. The circumference of knowledge was small, but the diameter of their fear was infinite. They peered into the night, fearing for the worst and looked for assistance, in whatever form it would carry. An unintelligible sound can be a voice, and when found, the cadence of its cry is enmeshed within the consciousness of the individual in the dark.

Life in that time was a waking dream, each step in life closer to lucid consciousness. Then one day, it is as if the cloudy film that permeated their retinas were dragged away, their vision finally in focus with their actual surroundings. For many years, evil did not have a face. Cave paintings changed that. Grunts and snarls were replaced with words and phrases. Once these ideas in the form of words were tied into thoughts, they stared into the wilderness, wondering the workings of this world. This transfiguration of thoughts was human's first enlightenment, a time of revolution. The revolution, in the end, was, unfortunately, nothing more than a masquerade, an achievement that allowed the Devil to enter the narrative. The doorway into the minds of these early Homo sapiens was fear. God did not create fear. The forces of nature did. Nature created man as well, via the mechanism of evolution, which in part uses movement vying for equilibrium, which I will explain below.

The fundamental mechanics of nature work using various forces such as gravity, electromagnetism, the strong force, and the weak force. However, all forces and motions on earth, except for objects at the quantum level, always endeavor to attain equilibrium. We can use this understanding as a thought experiment that would allow us to post dictate the creation of religion via fear.

Why do we have weather? We can talk about the effects of barometric pressure, jet streams and temperature variation on weather patterns, but the same effects of weather continue to occur. The constant to weather is that the precipitation and pressure levels are trying to achieve a level of equilibrium. This is known and understood in the scientific community.

However, the empirical evidence also declares that everything terrestrial endeavors to maintain equilibrium. Trees have large trunks and a deep root system to stabilize their position on earth. The thick branches grow outward but in an acute angle relative to the trunk so that they can withstand the force of gravity. This is an evolutionary change that attempts to maintain equilibrium. The accretion process that formed the earth into the oblate spheroid that it is today created a planet with a liquid mantle layer covered

Fear Brings About Religion

in a thin solid crust. The constant shifting of the parts of the crust, the tectonic plates, creates friction in certain areas, which form earthquakes and compressional forces, which result in mountain ranges. The pressures and movements of earth vie for equilibrium. The evolution of animals is based on a constant state of equilibrium. Changes to one animal will propagate throughout the food chain and the other inhabitants of this hierarchal tree will either adapt or become extinct. World and nation economics endure the repetitious and persistent peaks and valleys of prosperity and recessions, hoping for equilibrium in the markets.

The distinguishable feature of this thought experiment is that equilibrium is not achievable. It can never occur, in the terrestrial sense within a humanly tangible timeframe. The idea borrows from the law of inertia, in that an object that is in motion stays in motion.

In this same vein, since the creation of the universe started with a big bang, which is to say everything that exists in this universe began in a state of motion, the fact that equilibrium is impossible is in of itself an engine for perpetual motion. Since equilibrium is not possible, the underlying mechanic motions in trying to create this atmosphere of equilibrium is constant and is the fuel for all terrestrial movement, macroscopic forces, and evolution. Evolution would stop if all living things stopped changing.

Nevertheless, the inevitable change in animals, for example, is indistinguishable from the nuclear arms race of the Cold War. A predator becomes stronger, so to survive, the prey becomes faster. Do the predators gain better eyesight? The prey develops camouflage. A ceasefire within the animal kingdom is inconceivable, so the race continues. The motion of evolution is eternal, until all living things are dead, which may be an impossible feat. A perfect display of the vitality of living things is our ongoing search for life on Mars, a place that by all residents of the imagination is uninhabitable. There are lifeforms called tardigrades

Fear Brings About Religion

that can survive the vacuum of space; radiation doses hundreds of times higher than that which would kill a human and have a unique hibernation mechanism in that they dehydrate themselves for up to 30 years, then rehydrate and continue to survive. If evolution shaped the anatomy of this hearty "micro-animal," imagine the possibilities of a life form fashioned in the barren environment on Mars.

However, life not only evolves but can also bring forth new forms of "life," through the emergent property called consciousness. As life forms, we all are descendants of animals that evolved from even more primitive animals. These ancient living things were simple biological engines of locomotion, without fear to hinder them or protect them, depending on the side of the coin you land on. The life and death of these organisms were relegated to chance, to statistics by some form of primordial and somewhat sinister Egalitarianism. Evolutionary edges in life were scarce, but were still there, in some nominal form. As these beings strived to maintain survival, and in essence equilibrium with their surroundings, they were faced with certain situations that required split-second responses. Apart from apex predators, those that evolved beneficial reflexes as an instinct survived longer. These reflexes are the result of type I and type II errors, false positives, and false negatives. A typical false positive in the animal kingdom, hearing sounds or seeing sights, thinking that some predator is out to get you, even though there is nothing present and running away from that sight or sound, allowed these animals to statistically live longer and to procreate more frequently.

These emotionally blind individuals produced statistical quotients when the survivors of the cruel Darwinian world would give birth to offspring. The reflexes born by type 1 errors, after some time, became encoded in the genes of the offspring and their progeny in the form of instinct, due to their use for survival. Soon, these reflexes, combined with the emergence of thought created fear. Fear is the embodiment of a "run for your life" reflex, combined with consciousness. It is the personification of instincts to flee, handed down from generation to generation. Likewise, love is a derivative of a mammal's instinct to nurture, hardwired in the genes that created us. The remainder of the emotions we experience is also through the confluence of ancestral instincts and thoughts.

With the emotional framework fully established and a mind evolved that was cognizant of logical understanding, our predecessors strived to explain what they saw. Logic, in its most primitive iteration, was more about reconciliation and justification of emotions, rather than peering into the underlying architecture of the world, the gears that moved in the backdrop. When a basic answer to a specific situation could not be procured, events were tied to divine deities, beings that were supposedly much stronger than our ancestors were and therefore had answers to all of life's questions. At first, they were just stories told for enjoyment, but as generations passed, they became a place of solace for our fearful minds and became tangible and then required. They either existed for ages or were eternal beings. These entities, these gods, could unlock the secrets of life that we could not explain on our own. The passing down of these stories to their offspring were the first acts of indoctrination. Questions were asked, and they were given supernatural responses. Members of the tribe did not question these "answers" because their "trustworthy" parents or wise tribal elders told them. Why does it rain? A rain god commanded it. Why did a volcano erupt? Why did the earth quake? A god was angry. How do we stop a god from becoming angry? Offer a gift. These gifts of atonement ranged from grain and livestock offerings to human sacrifices. Human sacrifice was a staple of ancient worship and is still continuously used in modern religions, most specifically Christianity. More on that later.

Fear Brings About Religion

It is at this point when early man was cajoled into believing in the supernatural and the main ingredient in this recipe for future global fragmentation (besides language) was fear. The fear that saved us from the predators in Africa has now paralyzed our sense of logic and created safe spaces for our primitive understanding of celestial and terrestrial mechanics. These safe spaces have allowed these bogus myths time to mature and become part of the fabric of human culture. Once established, these stories were there to stay. They were to become a blemish on the tapestry of our fundamental understanding and to this day, there has still not been any way for us to cleanse ourselves from this enduring defect, the dried ketchup stain on the white shirt of our soul.

There was Anubis, the god of the dead and protector of graves. Seth was the god of disorder in the world and responsible for the chaos that purportedly engulfed the earth at the time. Poseidon commanded the to and fro of the oceans. Ceres is the goddess of fertility and agriculture and was to be honored at the time of the harvest. Thoth was the god of magic and the moon. They were the explanation for the unexplainable.

The interesting aspect of almost all gods (to my knowledge) is that they are mainly all android or gynoid in form or nature. Why is this? It is because we humans are visual. Imagery is the first language humans, and many vertebrate animals learn in life, instincts being involuntary and therefore not an actual language. This visual language is the conscious decoding of information of moving images. Emotions from a face, the sight of a lion, the birth of a baby, the image of a meal all evoke data that the brain arranges into understanding. There is more to the image than these freeze frames in time, but the brain understands the crossfire of information by combing out the weeds from the wheat. The pertinent information is assimilated, and the codified message is understood. The palpable color and textures are decoded bit by bit, in the same manner, a TIFF or BMP file stores information. Since we first learned in image format and we are accustomed to thinking of ourselves as higher beings, our egocentric selves personify that which we cannot comprehend, mainly the gods that we worship. We were not made in God's image. He was made in ours.

The final form in the evolution of this assimilating monster is the fusion of these archaic beliefs with new consecrated doctrine. Our ancestors constantly tried to corset these components into an ideology. Once the conditions were ripe for control and people began to have "faith," the parasite of religion was born. Religion, in the end, was a byproduct of the concatenation of ideas distilled from the lives lived by our ancestors. Does this mean I truly believe there is a biological parasite called religion? Of course not! The actual parasite is a mental Boolean logic gate system that subsumes information that you receive and alters it. It is a set of Pavlovian responses created by filtering the input you receive through the sieve of indoctrination.

A perfect example of how the parasite of religion can suspend logic in the mind of the infected is the Eucharist. The Roman Catholic Church teaches that the bread and wine, similar to what was used in the "Lords Supper" by the mythological Jesus, once consecrated by the Priest, converts into the flesh and blood of Jesus Christ himself. The transformation itself is accomplished by the miraculous act known as transubstantiation. As listed under the Catechism of the Catholic Church: *"The signs of bread and wine become, in a way surpassing understanding, the Body and Blood of Christ.'* The logical response to this information is that this is all nonsense. Bread cannot turn to flesh, more specifically the flesh of a person that has supposedly been dead for over 2,000 years and if it did, you would be guilty of cannibalism, which the Bible condemns! However, due to the reuptake of this stimulus by the faith parasite, parishioners have no problem with this belief! There

Fear Brings About Religion

is no diametrically opposing view to this belief. If you ask a Catholic directly, *"How can you believe such an idea,"* this believer will discharge reason and parrot *"Well. That's what I believe in."* If pushed further, they will simply ignore the logic of the questioning. This is what the parasite does to protect its host. More of this be discussed in the next chapter.

Why did fear bring about religion? This occurred because it was the natural progression of fear. It is the evolution of fear. It is the reason why religion may never be eliminated from our planet. It has been encoded in our soul, once we developed a consciousness. What would life be without fear? It would be the absence of life. Imagine the gazelle without fear of the lion; a succinct conclusion. Once we were able to couple instincts along with our consciousness, we decided we did not want to die. We wanted to live. We have jettisoned the split second instinct that governed our lives and started to walk because we wanted to. We decided to take that first step, out of our own initiative.

Once we started walking on our own accord, we had to look where we were walking. No longer compelled to move for survival, we were able to think. We were afforded the time to ponder. What is fear to a ponderer, a wanderer of thoughts? Fear is a lack of control of your next step, an absence of dominion over your surroundings. It is the capitulation of thoughts that freeze your mental faculties. It is a shortage of authority of your environment. This is the very embodiment of fear.

Once released from the extents of instincts, we not only can think about our environment, but we can also ponder introspectively. The attack from the predator that you always avoided can cause your death. Death is the end of your existence. Not good. Once you convolve those two ideas, true fear emerges. You want to live. Survival is now the most important objective and not because of Darwinian mechanics. It guides our thoughts.

Fear Brings About Religion

Somehow fear, the emotion that materialized with our emergent understanding of instinctual compulsion brought us back to the dark ages. We moved for survival again, but this time we thought about which path to take. The problem is that others did not think about which passage to cross. They allowed fear to guide them. The evolution of fear, as I will explain will not stop death but will constrain our lives so that we become pneumatized bones of our former selves. Our lives will become hollow. We turn to stories for comfort from this wicked world. These stories were the light at the end of the tunnel.

I remember the first time I went to a September 11th memorial. At night, there were two lights that were pointed to the sky, simulating the placement of the original twin towers. As we got closer by car, my wife and I, along with a former friend saw glitter swirling and emanating from the lights above. It looked like the initiation of a Star Trek transporter. It was only when I got out of the car and walked onto the makeshift road that I realized what made this spectacle so beautiful. There were thousands of insects, drawn to the lights. As I came closer to the lights, I saw these insects one by one travel to the base of the light fixture, only to be fried once they touched the bulb itself. They died because of their attraction to the light.

The terminally religious are all moths that came too close to a heated light bulb. They were compelled to follow the light. What is the light, in a human sense? It is the confluence of fear and promise. This is called hope. Hope is much more dangerous than fear, in the ontological sense. It can turn a protector of children into a suicide bomber. It can turn a savior into a martyr. It can draw men into drinking seawater when they are at their limits of thirst.

Hope is the stronghold of religion, but fear is its cornerstone. The parasite of religion cannot exist without fear as its impulse engine. However, once in motion, the parasite uses hope as its primary mechanism of integration. It makes a hopeless primate wonder about their surroundings and forces them to contemplate *"Is this all that there is to this world?" "Is there anything else beyond this?" "What about my children? Do they have a hope beyond this world of animals?"* The parasite feeds off the fear created by this longing for more and provides a dopaminergic reward. This reward comes in the form of belief in a life or world beyond the one they currently occupy. It stems from the belief that we are superior to animals in that we were created specifically for a purpose, not by sheer accident.

The pondering of oneself and of one's closest tribe in this dangerous world they find themselves in is what generates fear. Once this fear is codified into doctrinal rules, then religion is created. Fear is what keeps parishioners in line. Understand that fear equals power in religion and religious authority is an awesome power. The power of religion is that you may not be certain if you have followed the letter of the law, but the fear of imminent failure stops you from asking if you did. It is this fear that creates the perfect dormitory in the mind of the parishioner which allows religion to find and consume its host.

Chapter Three

Thought, like any parasite, cannot
exist without a compliant host.
- Bernard Beckett

Imagine that you have nothing. No food. No shelter. Your
health is fading. The clothes on your back are your only possessions.
Life is just a cyclical daily routine of being in anguish and living with
hunger, always looking for your next meal. Now, imagine that you
also have three children. How do you explain this constant state of
misery to them? You can't assure them that everything will be all
right in this world because you are aware of the hand you were dealt.
You are an unskilled worker looking for work that does not exist.
A life of unmitigated poverty awaits you all. Failure is imminent.
What do you say to your kids?

If you are in that position, the only thing you can do, other
than trying to better your situation is to provide comfort to your
children but how can that be done? What can you offer when your
plate is empty? What type of hope can you give when you have
nothing of value? The only thing that can be done is to provide
relief through the use of stories. *"Do you know that there is a*

person more powerful than anyone in this world, who created us and has a wonderful plan for us all?" you may say. *"He will wipe every tear from their eyes. There will be no more death or mourning or crying or pain, for the old order of things has passed away."* – Revelation 21:4.

So the seed is sown for religion. It is the hopelessness followed by consecutive hope. It is in this manner that religion finds a host. In the beginning, harmless stories were told to assuage fears and to provide comfort. These tales became more and more complex until the fables created rules that must be followed. Once this occurred, religion was born. What makes humans such a valuable host? It is the fact that humans can believe and *want* to believe. This can lead to vivid and fanciful outcomes.

The Republic of Iceland is a majestic island country that has landscapes that rivals the set of the movie "The Lord of the Rings." However, there is an interesting statistic hidden in its vista. According to The Atlantic magazine, *"In one 1998 survey, 54.4 percent of Icelanders said they believed in the existence of elves".* The belief is so pervasive that construction projects have been delayed, altered or terminated due to the belief that these invisible fairies, known as huldufólk (hidden people) must be consulted prior to alterations that may uproot their homes! How did it come to be that seemingly logical adults go through great pains to appease these imaginary beings? Where did the hidden people come from?

Legend has it that the existence of the huldufólk can be traced back to the very beginning with Adam and Eve. When God came to earth to speak to Eve, some of her children were dirty, and so she hid them from God and denied their existence. God, being omniscient, was well aware of the children so he declared *"What man hides from God, God will hide from man.'* With that command, the hidden people were created and had been hidden ever since.

Religion Finds A Host

This Christianization story was apparently enough to make half of a nation believe in elves and fairies, enough that construction efforts are affected and that stories of elves replacing children with changelings leave some Icelanders in fear!

If we find it silly that Icelanders coordinate construction efforts around invisible magical elves, then you must also find the beliefs of billions of people equally childish and nonsensical. Substitute elves for Santa or the tooth fairy and Icelanders with Americans and you have equally ludicrous claims. However, there are only a rare few that take these stories seriously. What happens in more serious situations? Now, substitute Santa for Allah and Americans with Muslims. This combination generates Sharia Law. Honor killings. Suicide bombers. Jihad. Completely logical when said to a Muslim fundamentalist but highly illogical once you proceed down the path of logic we started with Iceland. How many people have died in the name of Allah, a mythological creature? Change Muslims to Christians and replace Allah with God/Yahweh. How many people died in the crusades for no reason at all? How many millions of people have died in the name of any false deity?

What empowers religious fanatics to blow themselves up in the name of their God? Courage. If fear brings about religion, then courage is the driving force of religious fundamentalism. Why fear death when you have a God that can resurrect you? Life in the martyr battlefield would be tantamount to playing a video game such as Call of Duty. Once you die, fear not. You will respawn. Faith is the fuel of their courage and what makes humans the perfect host for the parasite known as religion.

Let us take a more banal cult. Jehovah's Witnesses are known for being a passive, non-political, antiwar group so who cares if they have a very unusual and nontraditional view of the Bible text! They irritate others with their door to door service, but in the end, it seems harmless. But they are fundamentalists. How does courage factor into this group and allows them to perform actions tantamount to suicide bombing?

As a recovering Jehovah's Witness, I am an authority on such matters. They have a strict policy against blood. Due to an interpretation of the Bible, Jehovah's Witnesses are forbidden to accept blood transfusions, even if it means certain death. If a member of their congregation commits a sin and does not repent or decided to leave the "truth," all connections with their Jehovahs's Witness friends would be severed. If you have Witness family members, you have lost those as well. If they see you in public, they will look right through you, as if you do not exist. If your child is sexually abused, you are dissuaded from informing the authorities. Informing the police will only bring reproach upon Jehovah's name. They have recently changed their stance on this topic officially, due to the current lawsuits but the unspoken rule is still in operation.

Picture how many people died unnecessarily due to their faith in an imaginary figure? How many families have been destroyed because of a text that was written in the bronze age? How many children have been sexually abused by Jehovah's Witnesses in high positions? How many more will be molested or raped because these Elders or Ministerial Servants (also known as Pastors and Deacons to the rest of Christianity) never answered for their crimes and had a vast field of children they could groom from a very young age? Imagine that one of those children were yours!

If you are a member of Jehovah's Witnesses, none of the aforementioned will bother you! Why? Because of your courage in God. The courage that no matter what happens in this world, you will be resurrected back to this planet once all of the wickedness has been cleansed by Jehovah. Please read the following excerpt from the Jehovah's Witnesses website to see how they use scriptural mythology to instill fear and "courage" in God

"The wisdom, courage, and faith Joshua showed must have strengthened the Israelites during the many years they fought to take the land of Canaan. They needed courage not only to fight in battle but also to obey God. Just before Joshua died, he told them: 'You must be very courageous to keep and to do all that is written in the book of the law of Moses by never turning away from it to the right or to the left.' (Joshua 23:6) We too need courage to obey Jehovah at all times, especially when humans tell us to do something that is against God's will."

What is *not* described in this article is that according to the religion, the consecrated group of elders at the top of the organization known as the Governing Body were installed there by God himself and therefore they need to follow all of *their* commandments as well! This is the "spoiled spiritual food" that is fed to all Jehovah's Witnesses. It is this reason why parishioners of this faith can allow a loved one to die or commit suicide by refusing blood transfusions, why they will not turn in pedophiles to the police and why they can mute all connections with their families. God has a plan for all of his faithful servants, and if you follow every jot and tittle, you with obtain everlasting life in an earthly paradise. They are no better than the Islamists that kill themselves knowing that their 72 virgins await them.

The parasite of religion can procreate in vast numbers quickly because of the fear our early ancestors felt in surroundings that emerged with their consciousness 100,000 years ago. Approximately 3,500 years ago, when human history was being written down, and the Abrahamic religion was taking a foothold in the fertile crescent, we can read the accounts of indoctrinated individuals that became hosts to this parasite and see how courage impelled this parasite to propagate to the entire world.

There were many religions before Judaism, but it is at this inception that we see the beginnings of the biggest scourge of our planet, the creation of the Abrahamic God. Fear was abundant at that time, and the indigenous Canaanites that suffered economically (conjectured by some historians and archeologists) moved to other areas to seek a better life. These stragglers wanted to form an identity to distance themselves from their previous lives and to provide a unifying order for the new tribe, the Israelites. It is here where the God Yahweh / Jehovah was created. They created a supernatural bodyguard that had the best interests of the tribe in mind, something that could cajole the clan to pompous prideful elevation due to their newfound nation. Their God requested reclamation of the Israelites property and armed with the courage promulgated by the backing of a supreme being, the wars began. At least they occurred in the Bible. According to people of authority, some of these battles never took place. Other conflicts may have occurred but not with the results as recorded in the Bible.

Why are humans predisposed to religion? What are the factors in humans that make them such great hosts? We have already expounded on fear and courage and how they affect an individual from a host standpoint. What about faith? What does faith do to a person? Faith is an interesting quality in that it requires many traits and emotions for it to engage upon an individual. It requires fear as the initial emotion a being feels when it realizes that it does not want to die. The stories heard from the original tribe elders provided hope for a future. This hope is essential for future faith. After these stories are instilled in their minds, it requires courage to act upon these fables and this courage, convolved with fear and hope, create belief. If belief is the confluence of all of these emotions and traits, then faith occurs when all logic is evacuated from this human cocktail. Believing in something from nothing is the very definition of faith.

It is faith that was the impulse engine for the Crusades, the Inquisition, the Nazi's Holocaust, and other atrocities. Faith is the motor that allows people to be complacent in their lives. Faith allows people to truly believe in miracles. Faith can make a father like the biblical Abraham place a knife onto the throat of his son. Faith can make a Jehovah's Witness withhold a blood transfusion for themselves or significant others when that is the only cure. Faith allowed 19 men to fly into the twin towers, the pentagon and an open field in Pennsylvania. Conversely, it was only facts that allowed the U.S. to kill Osama Bin Laden.

What does faith do to a person? How does it enslave the mind? A perfect example of faith gone wrong is the biblical Flood account. After the flood, the bible states that only eight people survived the incident. Is that enough for our species to have propagated to the magnitude that we see today? I tried to do the calculation, but none of them included death via accidental causes, natural disasters and genocide. It did not include the compounding of generations and also failed to take into account the sudden exponential growth rate, starting at the industrial revolution. Such a calculation is very complicated, so I went to www.worldometers.info/world-population/#pastfuture for answers. Using mathematical algorithms, trusted sources such as the U.S. Census Bureau and population milestones from historical archives it indicated that to conceive a society of our current size, there needed to be approximately 6.5 million people on earth at around 4,500 years ago.

This form of detective work illustrates the main point of contention with religion and science. As stated earlier, science evaluates a hypothesis through experimentation and peer review. Religion, on the other hand, decides what is true in the first place and then looks for scientific facts or any facts in general, to prop up its astonishing claims regardless how silly it may sound, an autonomic reverse thinking of sorts.

Religion Finds A Host

Faith allows a person to believe without evidence but with the courage to act. Faith allows a person to ignore medical help while providing tithe money or "seed" to a person of religious power hoping to be cured as in the Seed-Faith principle. Faith makes people believe that the universe was created by a divine being and that science is not needed, stunting the scientific knowledge of a parishioner. It is faith that allows a person to ignore the theory of evolution and believe in the creation myth represented in the bible. *"'If you can'?" said Jesus. "Everything is possible for one who believes."* - Mark 9:23.

Faith can also lead to hidden conflicts in an adherents thinking that are apparent to outside observers. We can all laud the fact that God stopped Abraham from killing Isaac, but we had no problem when God allowed Satan to kill the children of Job? *"While he was still speaking, yet another messenger came and said, "Your sons and daughters were feasting and drinking wine at the oldest brother's house when suddenly a mighty wind swept in from the desert and struck the four corners of the house. It collapsed on them, and they are dead, and I am the only one who has escaped to tell you!"* – Job 1:18-19.

A normal person who knew of the bargain God entered with Satan would have cursed God in that instant for taking their children away over a wager. However, a person of faith would ignore the action and look towards the ending when Job was blessed as if that paid for the suffering that Job went through. *"After Job had prayed for his friends, the LORD restored his fortunes and gave him twice as much as he had before. All his brothers and sisters and everyone who had known him before came and ate with him in his house. They comforted and consoled him over all the trouble the LORD had brought on him, and each one gave him a piece of silver[a] and a gold ring. The LORD blessed the latter part of Job's life more than the former part. He had fourteen thousand sheep, six* thousand camels, a thousand yoke of oxen and a thousand donkeys. And he also had seven sons and three daughters. The first daughter he named Jemimah, the second Keziah, and the third Keren-Happuch. Nowhere in all the land were there found women as beautiful as Job's daughters, and their father granted them an inheritance along with their brothers." – Job 42:10-15.

There was a situation once when I described to a Jehovah's Witness elder the disgust that I felt when God allowed the death of Job's children all because of a game He and Satan were playing. His response? "But at the end, Job was blessed two-fold! He ended up having another ten children!" I responded "Thank god you are not a parent! How do you think that being blessed with additional children makes up for the death of the previous children?" The stoic blank stare that he comfortably wore as I looked on in disgust was evidence enough that he still did not understand. Faith compelled this adult to conclude that God acted acceptably when it came to this drive-by murder!

If this sort of behavior is satisfactory with Christian parishioners, then anything goes. In the end, God watches the dust move on the wondrous blue pearl sitting on the tip of his finger, as the people submit to his every commandment.

Chapter Four

We humans are the greatest of earth's parasites.
- Martin H. Fischer

A parasite is an interesting life form. They can be independent living beings, but once in contact with a proper host, it will attach itself and use the host to acquire food or make the unknowing body a biological petri dish! The only requirement of a host is that the environment is healthy and robust for the parasite. It must fulfill a purpose. Propagation. Food consumption. Transmission. The best way of understanding how a parasite makes use of a host is to examine an example of parasitic inhabitation.

Tapeworm infections occur when a human or other animal ingests tapeworm eggs or larvae in raw or undercooked meat. Once this infected matter is consumed, it will attach itself to the intestines of a person. Since it does not have a mouth or digestive tract, it absorbs nutrients intended for its host through its semi-permeable surface membrane, robbing the human from its proper nourishment. Depending on the number of worms in the infected individual, one may suffer from diarrhea, anorexia and possible clogging of the digestive tract.

The Parasite Begins To Feast

This form of parasitic infection is relatively harmless compared to the bevy of other intruders. However, the general idea is established. An object connects to a host and uses the host for its wellbeing. This is exactly how religions machinations operate on an individual. Once the ideologies have been ingested, they take root in the "soul" and begin to assimilate and then override the emotions of the parishioner. The person no longer feels accomplishment over individual feats but entrusts these wonderful experiences to its Savior. Milestones in their mental development are relegated to God and not to its actions as a human being. This consumption of elicited emotions feed the parasite of religion, and in turn, it provides comfort to the host, in the form of ideological blessings.

The thoughts and ideas by themselves are not parasitic. It is the vehicle of religion that enables these ideas to evolve into a parasitic mode of life. It is not the thoughts or allusions of a higher being that is inherently harmful. It is the codification of this belief and the inclusion of faith and doctrine that converts these obscure concepts into a symbiotic mental parasite. This may sound hyperbolic in its assertion, but it is in no way intended to be inflammatory. Incendiary rhetoric does not assist in the goal of religious emancipation but is necessary when speaking the truth about this pervasive evil.

Religion in itself is a parasite of the mind, but like parasites, there are different variants. I will be focusing on the Judeo-Christian strain since that is the extent of my exposure. This type of parasite is unique in that it directly affects the mind of an individual. The actions of this person would be much different if not for the manipulatory infection of religion. There is a direct comparison of this illness, and it can be found in nature. It is called, informally, the zombie snail.

The Parasite Begins To Feast

Leucochloridium is a parasite that is eaten by snails when it ingests the droppings of an infected bird. The parasite secures itself to the liver of the animal and begins to tunnel into the eyestalks, also known as the snail's tentacles, where the photosensitive cells at the tip act as the eyes. Once the parasite branches out into the eyestalks, it creates a brood sac that will soon be full of larval parasites. The full sac resembles a caterpillar, pulsating in a greenish brown color. This is done, so birds will consider it to be a tasty snack and eat the eyestalks of the infected snail. However, snails are nocturnal, and birds that hunt for caterpillars or maggots are not. What happens next sounds surreal. Via a mechanism unknown at this time, possibly hormonal, it controls the mind of the snail and compels it to travel up to the top of the trees during the day. This forces the snail to confront its predator head on, without fear and allows itself to commit the ultimate sacrifice. This sacrifice is only in the head of the influenced snail, however. Once eaten, the life cycle of the parasite begins again.

The way religion operates is congruent to that of the zombie snail. Once religion takes hold of the mind of an individual, it begins to produce more parasites in the form of evangelical actions. This may be preaching, praying for others or actively talking about God in the workplace or with friends during a conversation. If a person catches the religious parasite from these pronouncements and allows it to develop, they will also become a host for the disease, and then they start to act differently. This illness develops many ways. *"Have you lost a loved one? Well, do you know that they are in heaven and you can see them again? Would you like to know how you can gain access to heaven as well?"* Another avenue could be through fear. *"Isn't this world such a wicked and immoral one? Doesn't it seem that there is a lack of respect for individuals? Have you noticed the constant wars, natural disasters, and illness that permeates the earth? God notices, and he has a plan for all of us, free of all of this pain and suffering, but only if we follow his commandments. To everyone else, hell awaits them. Would you like to know what that glorious plan is?"* The most insidious form of infection is via indoctrination of children.

Regardless of the variant you have been infected with, the most common and difficult symptom to deal with is the removal of your critical thinking instincts and the installation of indebted servitude to God. A hearty belief in God overrides your basic mental faculties and makes the discussion of opposing views impossible. This ensures that you remain infected. It also makes all parts of your very being subservient to God. All accolades belong to God. How many of us have heard *"Thank God I got a raise"* or *"God made my daughter beautiful"* or even *"It was only by the grace of God that I was able to endure such a trial."* How disgusting is it that none of the aforementioned instances could have been contributed to the person itself! Was it not the hard work, determination, and overtime that enabled you to receive a raise at work? Was it not the work of you and your mate that created the beautiful features of your daughter? Was it not the headstrong mental strength and fortitude that allowed you to overcome such an ominous and seemly insurmountable ordeal? Relegating all achievements to a heavenly father is disgraceful! It deprives us of everything that would make any normal human being happy.

Regardless of how obvious this mental phantasm operates, the sickness of religion has reached pandemic status. Religion is mainly responsible for most of the wars that have occurred. Apologists are quick to mention the combat, conflict and vast destruction imposed by Adolf Hitler as non-religious but fail to mention where he could have received these ideas from. He regularly invoked the name of Jesus in his pronouncements. He held Jesus in high regard, calling him an "Aryan fighter" against the Jewish establishment, so he was obviously familiar with the Bible. Antisemitism? Was it not

The Parasite Begins To Feast

the Christians who stated that the Jews were the ones who initiated the crucifixion of Jesus at Golgotha and that they had to pay? Ethnic cleansing? Is it not in the Old Testament that we see the mass genocides of the Midianites, Amalekites and the Amorites, done by command from God himself? Why should we feel like Adolf Hitler is such an evil person when all of our biblical heroes would today be considered psychopaths and utter lunatics due to the genocide they imparted and would make a modern-day Son of Sam green with envy! I am in no way defending Adolf Hitler or condoning the gross atrocities he inflicted but please, let us call a spade a spade. If we glorify the bible stories of King David, Solomon, Jephthah or Joshua, you should effectively have no problem celebrating the barbarism of Adolf Hitler.

More importantly, if we believe that the Lord is righteous, moral and just, then the logical conclusion we must be compelled to comprehend is the realization that Hitler did nothing wrong! Please think about that. Let the following utterances marinate in your minds. What did Hitler do that God did not do? Mass genocide? Infanticide? The subjugation of people? The consignment of their innate moral values and the assignment of written ones? Selecting a chosen race of humans that would inherit this earth after the destruction of the remaining evil human race? God has done all of these things! What is so special about Hitler? There's no adjective significantly exclusive to either individual. If this is the case, then there should be no reason why we shouldn't worship Hitler himself. As radical as that may sound, there is no difference between the worship of either entity. Both make authoritative declarations that are false and as hollow as the morals they follow.

Now step back and realize that a religion with Hitler as the deity *was* attempted. It was called Nazism. We all know how that turned out. The result was so odious and abhorrent that an innocent ancient symbol known as the swastika, a symbol for God and peace has now been stigmatized into the emblem of racism and hatred. We are still, three-quarters of a century after the end of its dramatic conclusion, recovering from the depression of morality inflicted upon the fabric of society.

It is also interesting to note that the parasite of religion affects women differently. There is an additional level of subservience added. They are to be in submission to their husbands and all males in general. This is factual. The very fact that the world needed to have a women's rights movement attests to the very effect this parasite has on females. This movement was required because according to the Bible, women were nothing more than chattel. They were held as inferior beings, on the same datum line as animals and slaves.

Speaking of inferiority, let us discuss the asymmetrical organization of power when it comes to women. If you look back at our predecessors, Ancient Hominids, there are some conjectural arguments that the women were in charge of the group. Even some tribes today keep this structural nomenclature. If this was the case, you have a great argument for writing the bible. In effect, it was most probably a coup by men to overtake the overarching position of maternal members, disenfranchising them and making them subservient on the basis of religious grounds. Purely speculation.

This thinking of submissive prostration to a deity subsumes all ideas into a compact pill of understanding called religion, the capsule of the manipulative parasite. These ineffable ideas cannot be watered down with psychological adulterants. They are distilled with the lens of religiosity. Humans are instilled with an instinctual predilection towards religion, due to the evolution of our thinking. Infected people appreciate the psychological safety net provided by religion and the false conflation of happiness and "truth."

The Parasite Begins To Feast

Religion is a means to happiness. This is the consensus among all faithful ones. They say that being close to God can only bring peace. They have not read the Bible and heard the pain and torture Job was subjected to, regardless of the propitiations he made upon Jehovah. The parasite of religion also has an added benefit of masking the obvious denigration of human values and emotions. Jehovah/Yahweh *allowed* Satan to torture Job; his only qualifier being that he must not be killed. All this and Job was highly faithful to God. *"In the land of Uz there lived a man whose name was Job. This man was blameless and upright; he feared God and shunned evil."* - Job 1:1. Let's not search our feelings to answer questions, for midi-chlorians are only fantasy. Let us use the Bible for what it is supposed to be, a teaching tool of history and how we should serve his Grace.

The result of all of this torture due to his perseverance? New kids, livestock, etc. *"The Lord blessed the latter part of Job's life more than the former part. He had fourteen thousand sheep, six thousand camels, a thousand yoke of oxen and a thousand donkeys. And he also had seven sons and three daughters. The first daughter he named Jemimah, the second Keziah, and the third Keren-Happuch. Nowhere in all the land were there found women as beautiful as Job's daughters, and their father granted them an inheritance along with their brothers. After this, Job lived a hundred and forty years; he saw his children and their children to the fourth generation. And so Job died, an old man and full of years."* - Job 42:12-17

But what did Job have to say to God for the dispersion of gifts from above? He had to grovel. *"Then Job replied to the Lord: "I know that you can do all things; no purpose of yours can be thwarted. You asked, 'Who is this that obscures my plans without knowledge?' Surely I spoke of things I did not understand, things too wonderful for me to know."* - Job 42:1-3. Things too wonderful to understand? Does Job have anywhere near a 1% capacity of understanding that we as modern human beings have? Is this knowledge too unfathomable for our acquisition? He also had to curse himself. *"You said, 'Listen now, and I will speak; I will question you, and you shall answer me.' My ears had heard of you, but now my eyes have seen you. Therefore, I despise myself and repent in dust and ashes."* - Job 42:4-6. Despise himself and repent in dust and ashes? Is this what our Lord and Savior need to hear? And for what? For God to undo the damage that he did? *"After Job had prayed for his friends, the Lord restored his fortunes and gave him twice as much as he had before. All his brothers and sisters and everyone who had known him before came and ate with him in his house. They comforted and consoled him over all the trouble the Lord had brought on him, and each one gave him a piece of silver and a gold ring."* - Job 42:10-11. In clear verbiage, it states that God himself brought the trouble upon Job. It was his doing. How can religion, the Christian religion, in this case, be a receptacle that promulgates love and happiness when the God that is the center of religious understanding uses Satan the Devil, the *"father of the lie"* (John 8:44) as an instrument in his cause! Lucifer, the one that humans pray to God for protection from is a tool in the workshop of Yahweh! These are not *my* words. This is what the holy inscriptions compel you to understand!

With this single example of abuse by the Lord Almighty, it is obvious that religion cannot be a means for happiness. But people claim that it brings peace and is a source for love, an obvious symptom of this religious parasite. The simple explanation for this paradoxical thinking is that they have never read the bible! They know nothing about the true God, other than the cherry-picked nonsensical drivel that propagates the pews from the church pulpits. If Satan is the father of the lie, then his sons have infiltrated the sacred holy places, no doubt with assistance from Yahweh himself!

There are many ways that religion does not lead to happiness but to trauma forced indebted servitude and fear of reprisal. They vary on which religion or cult you are affiliated with and the degree of immersion with regards to your religiosity. Fundamentalists, who take the Bibles words to heart and believe all of the inspired words with infinitesimal voracity are affected differently than religious moderates, who have faith based off of their feelings which leads them to fallacious and senseless points of view. In many respects, what is formulated is a construct that punishes you for not following certain guidelines, depending on your religion or cult following. This mental theological scarring, a spiritual lobotomy in some respects creates a force field around religious patrons, inhibiting their escape and if their liberation from the church is successful, they are altered, possibly for all time. This is no different than what war veterans experience once they return from the world and find themselves in a home that now appears to be foreign. Worshippers either stay in their place or suffer from PTSD, Post Traumatic Stress Disorder.

How does this work and why does it happen? Fundamentalists are the easiest to explain. They are quite capricious and can be inherently terse in their responses and rebuttals when they feel their convictions are under attack. This occurs because they are taught, since *only fundamentalists read* the Bible, that they cannot trust people who either question their faith, are apostates or critical thinkers. As we said before, the Bible itself claims to be inspired by God, so all religious facts are, pardon the pun, taken for gospel. The heads of these churches know this so with the same cherry picking skills farmers have, they look for fruit that will satisfy their customers. Tithes and donations are big business so pastors, priests, elders, etc. will find the best scriptures to keep their yearning constituents in their seats. You cannot make money if the pews are not full!

The perverse psychology of religion best works in a cultish environment, but it is important to note that the Bible ascribes to this mode of thinking. However, there is more to the mind manipulation than negative feedback. There is the dark pheromone of religious "Social Compliance" at work as well, and this mysterious phenomenon is part of an age-old technique known as mentalism. The best example of this effect that I am aware of is Derren Brown's "Pushed To The Edge." I highly recommend everyone to watch that effect. It is quite amazing the things people will do when the psychology of "Social Compliance" is introduced and used to its fullest potential. In a nutshell, the magician succeeds in making a person push another real live person off a ledge, in effect committing murder. Now, it does not start this way. The person is first given some small harmless menial tasks that will make them go against their innate conscience. These small tasks turn into larger tasks and then once this person is caught in a web of lies, after a series of situations it culminates into pushing another human being off the edge of a building. It is very important to remember that the majority of people who are in this situation *do* push the live person. This psychological mechanism of compliance works. It just needs to be scripted perfectly. Primer words are used, comfort provided when needed, persistence in acts when required and orders given when obedience is necessary.

This is exactly what religion uses to compel its parishioners to obey. It is important to note that although this applies more to fundamentalists, it is also applicable to the "Sunday Christian." For the complete effect, I'm going to use the Jehovah's Witnesses religion for this demonstration, since I was indoctrinated as one since birth and I know its inner workings intimately. It starts with small incremental situations, and before all is said and done, you blatantly do things that trespass your very humanity. The incarnate desire to do what is moral is shoveled into the abyss of religious corruption, and the self-depreciation of an individual is all that is left.

After a person has made their way into the Jehovah's Witnesses church (also known as a kingdom hall or congregation), the mental imprinting of doctrinal understanding begins. The pleasant things are taught first, in a personal book study. It is expressed that the current wicked condition of the world was not the intention of the creator. It is because of the disobedience of the first human couple that this state of imperfection exists. However, God has a plan for all of his followers to be resurrected into an earthly paradise, the same paradise our initial forefathers, Adam and Eve lived in. These future converts are also told that God has a personal name and that his name is Jehovah. These are the first primer phrases that are used to draw the person in. It shows that although humanity is primarily responsible for all sin and death, if a person follows God, all of this suffering will be removed. They also add a personal connection to God and humanize him by sharing his "personal name," Jehovah. With these ideas implanted, they move on to other various topics that reinforce the fact that God has the power to make everything perfect again, restoring the earthly paradise that was lost due to the first sin. Once these ideas have been fully consecrated into the mind of the individual, the truly sinister work begins. They are then taught that God has chosen a particular organization that channels all of the spiritual food that God provides and acts as the sole channel of God. The Witnesses show that the very books, pamphlets and even the bible that was given to them, free of charge were provided by this organization. They use the parable of the faithful and discreet slave, stated by Jesus in the Gospel to confirm this ideology. It is now also introduced that people who are not of Gods fold are worldly and will try to infect your mind with false propaganda. You are told that the bible you were given by the organization is the only true translation and that others should not be read. You should not read any other religious information from now on. These web of lies culminates to the point that you reach formal baptism. It is very important to read carefully the two questions you are forced, in front a large crowd to agree to with a resounding yes before you are formally baptized. It is the second question that clothes the nefarious injunction in the guise of following God.

(1) On the basis of the sacrifice of Jesus Christ, have you repented of your sins and dedicated yourself to Jehovah to do his will?

(2) Do you understand that your dedication and baptism identify you as one of Jehovah's Witnesses in association with God's spirit-directed organization?

Once you have been baptized, it is too late. Now that you are under the umbrella of the "Organization," doctrines that were not robustly discussed before now appear in the forefront. You cannot accept a blood transfusion, even if it means certain death. Anything that *God's spirit-directed organization* states in their articles, no matter how controversial, must be followed. You must preach a certain number of hours (minimum) as a male if you would like to move up in the congregation's hierarchy. If you sin and do not repent, you will be disfellowshipped.

"But now I am writing to you that you must not associate with anyone who claims to be a brother or sister but is sexually immoral or greedy, an idolater or slanderer, a drunkard or swindler. Do not even eat with such people." - 1 Corinthians 5:11.

This means that anyone who is a Jehovah's Witness, even members who are family or best friends can no longer talk to you due to your mandatory expulsion from the church. They must act like you do not exist. The only way to gain your familial counterparts back is to repent so that you become reinstated into the cultish organization.

In the original example, Derren Brown was able to make a person push a live human being off a building, to their death. Being fully indoctrinated in the Jehovah's Witness religion will allow the organization to effectively blackmail you into complete indebted servitude to their organization or suffer the complete severance of the people you love most and if the opportunity presents itself, allow yourself or your child to die because of the refusal of a blood transfusion. Two sides of the same coin.

What about a religion that is not as radical? The comparisons are not as self-evident, but the mechanisms are still in place, albeit in a more subtle manner. Our next example will be that of orthodox Christianity, the variants known as Catholicism and Protestantism. Let's dispense with the indoctrination aspect of acquiring the mainstay faith and see how this parasite operates in a more moderate atmosphere. People who take shelter from inquisitors using their churches cleric as theological barracks respond quite differently when induced into extemporaneous conversations without their epistemological crutches. They walk differently. They may not truly believe in hellfire or the inevitable accession into heaven, no matter how you broker the situation, but one of the most adjudicated conclusions that all parishioners and clergymen agree on is that the human soul is implanted the instant the new being is conceived. How could such a banal belief have an impact on others?

Cancer in of itself is a devastating illness that can affect anyone, due to the mechanisms of evolution. Cells that divide more often thrive. However, a controlled division is built into the construction of every living thing. There are cells that in effect commit suicide when necessary, due to the blueprints of the machine schematics of the being, such as the spaces between the fingers and toes. During embryonic development, cells exist between these areas, but because certain appendages are coded as required physically by the DNA of the animal, cell death is required to create separations. Normal health occurs when natural cell division and death are maintained in a controlled state. Cancer develops when cells abnormally divide.

There are many treatments for cancer with varying degrees for success depending on the type of treatment used and the type of cancer itself. Radiation therapy uses ionizing radiation to initiate cell death of the malignant tissues. However, healthy tissue can be damaged as well with this treatment. There is another treatment called "stem cell transplants." This method can either help you recover from radiation therapy, by helping your body restart your stem cell production process or attack the cancer itself.

The issue with using stem cells is that essentially, you need to harvest human embryos. Enter the epistemological argument. Does a human's life begin at the point of conception? At once you will realize that the only reason for the dammed progress of this medicinal treatment is religion. So, could such a banal belief like the soul being infused into an embryo have an impact on others? Certainly so.

Once all your moral constraints are abrogated to the lord, the human is a mere shell of their former selves even if they were blessed with life before being indoctrinated into the faith. There is no escaping the fact that this illness is usually chronic and few have forced it into the path of regression.

The parasite will make you sick and will try to keep you in its clutches, but there is an even more sinister mechanism in play when it comes to religion. Some humans have been affected by the parasite and then took it upon themselves, through parasitic persuasion, to redefine morality and ensure that the sacred text align perfectly with current scientific evidence. The label for these individuals is apologists.

These proponents for religion allow the revoltingly obtuse concepts prescribed by writings like the bible to proliferate within civilizations without contempt. The efficiency in which they execute their directive is striking. They have overwhelming influence over the primary group, the cleric class and have infiltrated every religion that I am aware of. The Catholic Church has an unbroken chain of apologists, known as popes that began with Jesus himself, the so-called great emancipator of the filth known as the Old Testament. This is far from an exaggeration. Read the following scriptures below regarding the murder of King David's son and the subsequent apologetic exchange to see the double jointed arguments at work.

"Why have you despised the word of the LORD by doing evil in His sight? You have struck down Uriah the Hittite with the sword, have taken his wife to be your wife, and have killed him with the sword of the sons of Ammon. " However, because by this deed you have given occasion to the enemies of the LORD to blaspheme, the child also that is born to you shall surely die." So Nathan went to his house. Then the LORD struck the child that Uriah's widow bore to David, so that he was very sick. Then it happened on the seventh day that the child died." - 2 Samuel 12:9, 14-15 & 18.

Excerpts from an apologetic argument from www.apologeticspress.org:

David's adulterous relationship with Bathsheba is one of the most infamous, heartbreaking events recorded in the Old Testament. The emotional pain and anguish caused by David's sin plagued the king for the remainder of his days. In the midst of the biblical record concerning God's dealing with David's sin, skeptics believe they have found a legitimate moral complaint against the God of the Bible (Wells, 2001). Upon reading this text, the skeptic suggests that God is unjust for killing an innocent child. How could a loving God kill an innocent child? The skeptic further suggests that this passage proves that God showed favoritism to David, because Leviticus 20:10 says that, under the Law of Moses, a man who committed adultery with another man's wife should be killed. Why was it the case that David was not killed for his adultery, when the Old Testament commanded that adulterers should be killed? One plausible reason is that there was a stipulation placed on the death sentence for those who committed adultery. In order to sentence adulterers to death, a minimum of two witnesses had to present evidence against the accused. Deuteronomy 17:6 says: "Whoever is worthy of death shall be put to death on the testimony of two or three witnesses, but he shall not be put to death on the testimony of one witness." In the case of David and Bathsheba, no witnesses came forward to testify against them. In fact, the text indicates that the only reason Nathan knew about the incident was miraculous revelation from God. In short, there is no biblical indication that the minimum of two human witnesses could not be found to testify against David (see Miller, 2003). Mosaic Law would not include God's omniscient ability as testimony, thus, David would not have been condemned by the Law of Moses. How, then, can an infinitely loving God cause the death of innocent children and still be considered loving? The skeptic simply says that if it is true that God caused the death of innocent babies, then it is impossible for a moral person to consider that God as loving. The skeptical argument goes something like this: (1) A good and loving God would not kill innocent children; (2) the God of the Bible kills innocent children; (3) therefore the God of the Bible cannot be good and loving. At first glance, this logic seems to make sense. When examined more closely, however, there lies within this argument a faulty assumption. The faulty assumption built into this line of reasoning is that the death of an innocent child is always, in every circumstance, evil. ... In summary, it is the case that God treated David in perfect accord with the Law of Moses, showing no partiality. Furthermore, it has been shown that since death is not inherently evil, God was not guilty of immorality by causing the child's death. God also ushered David's son into an eternity of bliss. Therefore, the skeptic's charge against God fails once again to discredit His infinitely flawless character. As Abraham asked the rhetorical question in the long ago, "Shall not the Judge of all the earth do right?" (Genesis 18:25). The answer has been the same throughout the millennia—a resounding "Yes."

This is what an argument from an infected individual looks like. Please reread the biblical text and then the apologist's refutation. See the underlying mechanics at work.

Religion is the only discipline that I know of that requires, better yet, necessitates and mandates the use of apologists. Without these word benders, religion could not have survived modern times. Review the aforementioned apologetic statement again. Visualize the arduous epistemological gymnastics required to reframe these archaic ideas into something more palpable, understanding that those were just excerpts! Understand the flexibility being used to mold disgusting but telling phrases in the bible into stories of sterling righteousness. See how the biblical schemes are stretched to contort to contemporaneous views with monomaniacal vigor. They are necessary to make this bible story moral.

Regardless of the spin that is put to this story, how can the murder of a faultless infant be moral? How can the life of a child be recompense for all of the sins of a normal thinking adult? More importantly, is the Bible truly moral?

Chapter Five

Morality binds people into groups. It gives us tribalism,
it gives us genocide, war, and politics. But it also
gives us heroism, altruism, and sainthood.
- Jonathan Haidt

"When they came toward the crowd, a man approached him,
knelt down to him, and said: 'Lord, have mercy on my son, because
he is an epileptic and is ill. He falls often into the fire and often into
the water. I brought him to your disciples, but they could not cure
him.' In reply Jesus said: 'O faithless and twisted generation, how
long must I continue with you? How long must I put up with you?
Bring him here to me.' Then Jesus rebuked the demon, and it came
out of him, and the boy was cured from that hour." - Matthew
17:14–18. According to the aforementioned scripture, epilepsy is
caused by demonic possession! A plausible concept in Iron Age
Palestine.

If an almighty being has commissioned the writing of a book
that would dictate the history of human civilization and outlined

its path to redemption, it is safe to surmise that it would be free from defect and misconceptions. However, whether you are reading the Bible, Koran, Talmud or the Vedas, it is obvious that mistakes abound. Now, people may say that the Bible, for example, was written long ago, before such things were discovered by the scientific method. However, this excuse cannot be tolerated. Its religious elders should be castrated from power for that very declaration! A god, a creator of everything that exists and designer of our own human bodies, would clearly understand without fail the inner workings of everything, regardless of what time the humans were 'inspired' to write his revelations. We need to impeach the idea that an all-inclusive source singlehandedly created and then propagated humans, animals, plants, planets, stars, galaxies and universes. We need to regard science as the medicine required for the spiritual adherent, a service dog of sorts for the blind religious parishioner. As we wipe the surface of this theology with topical antiseptic awaiting the injection of truth, please remember that although the arguments will be staunchly within the Christian realm, these disputations work in the cluttered confines of all religions. I provide this corrective measure from a Christian viewpoint, only because of my exposure to it.

When a person is sick, the treatment they receive is contingent on what ails them. If your sickness is bacterial, you will receive antibiotic medication to fight the illness. If viral, the best form of treatment is prevention, in the form of vaccines. The rise of antiviral medications for some ailments has been very helpful. As far as parasites are concerned, however, sometimes there are no medications that can help. The best form of a cure for symbiotic organisms, in general, is to disrupt the favorable conditions of the host, thereby affecting the parasite indirectly. The parasite remains living in its host because it benefits from this relationship. If we remove all of its benefits, the parasite will die. This mode of thinking is exactly what guides my offensive advances when discussing religion with someone. I look to decouple the mental relationship between the mind of the individual and the parasite of religion. Once that connection has been severed, the healing can begin. The method I use is quite direct, so I apologize for the bitter tone that this chapter and subsequent chapters may contain.

The etiology of a god can be traced back, as we have discussed previously, to the inquisitive yet ignorant early homo sapien. They, upon having a full grasp of imagination and a small helping of language, decided to explain all the mysteries of the world, such as the beginning of time, creation, our journey, and eventual destination. However, the capitulation to such ideas, as comforting yet primitively esoteric as they may be, are quite harmful. They do not lie in the realm of fact, as it becomes blatantly apparent when going through the religious assertions being made by its doctrinal constituents. Its ideas are ideological red herrings to the truth. We will attack each of these basic religious tenets in order of importance, starting with morality in this chapter.

Morality. It is the bookbinding of the Bible; the very hinge on which every scripture is hung on, or so we are taught to believe. If we glean upon the many stories it tells, we will stumble across many tales that are subscribed by bible thumpers as moralistic in value. If we allowed ourselves to don their spiritual blinders, we would agree with them. We would be okay with the raping, murdering and taking of slaves by the Israelites, Gods chosen people. There would be no problem with the pseudo-passion of Job. Abraham's quasi-sacrifice would be viewed as a morally upright circumstance. If you are a theist, the purpose of this chapter is to reason you out of something you had no reason to believe in the first place. If you are already on the fences, I look to burn down that structure.

Like a divine carpenter (let the reader use discernment), theologians use their spiritual shims to fill in the gaps with god in areas where their blueprint, the Bible, has no answers for. Where there are incorrect statements in the Bible, God's followers will fabricate truth, in a manner such as *"the facts presented to be truthful cannot be true because they cannot be harmonized with the Bible,"* a standard religious non-sequitur. They then tread, in masked trepidation, into waters they claim science has no dominion over. Morality is a typical area where they make spurious claims. They insist that without the Bible, we as humans would not know morality. Ignore the philosophical argument for the time being. Let's ask ourselves, is the bible moral? What would Job say?

"There was a man in the land of Uz whose name was Job. He was an upright man of integrity; he feared God and shunned what was bad. Seven sons and three daughters were born to him. His livestock amounted to 7,000 sheep, 3,000 camels, 1,000 cattle, and 500 donkeys, along with a very large number of servants, so that he became the greatest of all the people of the East." - Job 1:1-3.

So begins one of the greatest stories orated in the bible — one of the greatest, in the epistemological sense. We find that above the firmament of the terrestrial world, there is much deliberation between the Almighty Christian god Yahweh/Jehovah and his arch-nemesis, Satan the Devil.

'Now the day came when the sons of the true God entered to take their station before Jehovah and Satan also entered among them. Then Jehovah said to Satan: "Where have you come from?" Satan answered Jehovah: "From roving about on the earth and from walking about in it.". - Job 1:6-7

Logic As Medicine - Morality

This shows that although Satan, already having turned humanities first couple against God, is still allowed access in God's heavenly chambers! Yahweh facetiously poses as a question how great his servant Job is.

'And Jehovah said to Satan: "Have you taken note of my servant Job? There is no one like him on the earth. He is an upright man of integrity, fearing God and shunning what is bad." - Job 1:8

This is the all knowledgeable God asking the king of demons, knowing that he was the instigator of the "original sin" if he has noticed his fine subject, in essence instigating an attack.

'At that Satan answered Jehovah: "Is it for nothing that Job has feared God? Have you not put up a protective hedge around him and his house and everything he has? You have blessed the work of his hands, and his livestock has spread out in the land. But, for a change, stretch out your hand and strike everything he has, and he will surely curse you to your very face." - Job 1:9-11

Satan, accepting Gods call to arms, asks Yahweh for permission to unleash his unbridled rage upon this uninformed victim, to prove, in front of all of the angels in the assembly, that he was capable of turning Job against his supreme object of worship.

'Then Jehovah said to Satan: "Look! Everything that he has is in your hand. Only do not lay your hand on the man himself!" So Satan went out from the presence of Jehovah.' - Job 1:12

Satan then unleashes his restricted fury upon Job's children, servants, and livestock, killing them all, except for three servants, to relay the messages of what occurred to Job. When Satan returns to the halls of the spiritual courtroom, he is further enticed by Yahweh to test Job and then, via God's approval, struck Job with a malignant boil which covered his entire body!

The story continues, but the point has already been proven. How is this story moral? It shows that behind the blue silk curtain of the sky, back door dealings occur between good and evil for the most childish of purposes. It also shows that everyone on earth is dispensable, even faithful ones. We are merely props for our Gods play, whose narrative is to show to the world that humanity will worship him, regardless of the circumstances. How many people must endure the great winepress of God's wrath, their apparent sins sieved through the filter provided by their spiritual sommelier to extract the sediment accreted in this system of things! Original sin is the extrusion of the terrestrial appetites bestowed by God himself; which to me, on a separate note, provides solace but great pain and no relief because I feel like I am putting my own dog to sleep. Having been raised out of the ground from birth for the Lord's harvest as a Jehovah's Witness, yet delayed by the frost of this current world, I have come to realize that the great thaw of the late 1800s was forged by millennialism and not God, and is another form of control via the instrument of fallacy.

The moralistic value of its counterpart fable, the tale of Original Sin which occurred at the Garden of Eden holds the same currency. In a striking but veiled allusion of the Job story, we can see the distinct parallels but different dimensions of the characters and variables. Eve coveted the fruit. Satan the servant. Yahweh put the first human couple to the test using Satan as his instrument and then subsequently allowed Satan to test Job. Are these parallels purely coincidence? One should say yes if they are religious, for the bible states that *"All Scripture is inspired of God and beneficial for teaching, for reproving, for setting things straight, for disciplining in righteousness"* in 2 Timothy

3:16. However, this is not true! These two stories are tied to the same main vein of thought. Why? Because the bible was written by man without any assistance from its great creator because there is no God. We can read these stories because these provincial philistines, the ancient Israelites who are truly disingenuous Canaanites decided to create their own ethos and used these stories to describe their lensing of reality.

Let us continue with the subject of morality. When King David became infatuated with a woman named Bathsheba, who was married, he sent her husband, Uriah, a member of Israel's armed forces, to the front line of the battlefield to secure his death! This despicable manner of behavior must face retribution, but what would be the moral way of handling these matters of adultery, conspiracy, and murder? Should King David be put to death? Should David and his newfound love be forced to separate? No! According to the Bible, the moral way of handling such demonstrative neglect for human life would be to kill off his unborn son! *"Why did you despise the word of the LORD by doing what is evil in his eyes? You struck down Uriah the Hittite with the sword and took his wife to be your own. You killed him with the sword of the Ammonites." "But because by doing this you have shown utter contempt for the LORD, the son born to you will die."* - 2 Samuel 12:9 & 14. So, the correct and moral punishment is that David's son, who has yet to be born and sin, must die for the actions of his father! *"On the seventh day the child died."* - 2 Samuel 12:18. Morality at its finest ladies and gentlemen! Who says that God does not approve of abortion! The fact that he was involved in the abortion procedure ex utero is no reason for consolation or theological cover. No, I must submit to you that the roaring engine of hatred that is God, provided an outline of how to administer compensation on the ever tilting broken scale of morality. This is an immoral and deplorable action! In what world, other than the false dystopia painted with the brush of godly sovereignty, is this action moral!

While on the subject of the anointed King David, is it moral to kill someone for committing a sin that was not premeditated but was the result of an instinctual impulse? *"David again brought together all the able young men of Israel—thirty thousand. He and all his men went to Baalah in Judah to bring up from there the ark of God, which is called by the Name, the name of the Lord Almighty, who is enthroned between the cherubim on the ark. They set the ark of God on a new cart and brought it from the house of Abinadab, which was on the hill. Uzzah and Ahio, sons of Abinadab, were guiding the new cart with the ark of God on it, and Ahio was walking in front of it. David and all Israel were celebrating with all their might before the Lord, with castanets, harps, lyres, timbrels, sistrums and cymbals. When they came to the threshing floor of Nakon, Uzzah reached out and took hold of the ark of God, because the oxen stumbled. The Lord's anger burned against Uzzah because of his irreverent act; therefore God struck him down, and he died there beside the ark of God."* - 2 Samuel 1:1-6. This is a person acting on sheer instinct stopping the ark from falling, being struck down by God instantly for his apparent transgression. If a water-filled vase were tilting precariously from an end table and were about to topple onto the carpeted floor, you would do all you could to stop this action, and you would do it instinctually!

In addition to this, David had two sons at the time, Ammon and Absalom. The messianic lineage could have continued. Jesus did not need to descend from King David, just from the house of

David which does not preclude a bloodline of earthly sovereignty that is required by the Messiah. David's death for his appalling crimes could have been a perfectly plausible punishment.

In another fable, the Bible describes a person who wickedly sacrificed their own children to the god Molech. *"And you shall not let any of your children pass through the fire to Molech, neither shall you profane the name of your God: I am the LORD."* – Leviticus 18:21. What about the sacrifice of his only son that Abraham was compelled to make to God? *"Sometime later God tested Abraham. He said to him, "Abraham!" "Here I am," he replied. Then God said, "Take your son, your only son, whom you love—Isaac—and go to the region of Moriah. Sacrifice him there as a burnt offering on a mountain I will show you." Early the next morning Abraham got up and loaded his donkey. He took with him two of his servants and his son Isaac. When he had cut enough wood for the burnt offering, he set out for the place God had told him about. On the third day, Abraham looked up and saw the place in the distance. He said to his servants, "Stay here with the donkey while I and the boy go over there. We will worship and then we will come back to you." Abraham took the wood for the burnt offering and placed it on his son Isaac, and he himself carried the fire and the knife. As the two of them went on together, Isaac spoke up and said to his father Abraham, "Father?" "Yes, my son?" Abraham replied. "The fire and wood are here," Isaac said, "but where is the lamb for the burnt offering?" Abraham answered, "God himself will provide the lamb for the burnt offering, my son." And the two of them went on together. When they reached the place God had told him about, Abraham built an altar there and arranged the wood on it. He bound his son Isaac and laid him on the altar, on top of the wood. Then he reached out his hand and took the knife to slay his* son. But the angel of the LORD_called out to him from heaven, "Abraham! Abraham!" "Here I am," he replied. "Do not lay a hand on the boy," he said. "Do not do anything to him. Now I know that you fear God, because you have not withheld from me your son, your only son." " – Genesis 22:1-12.

One can argue that he would have reluctantly sacrificed his son, but he would have killed him if not for Gods last minute sacrificial reprieve. That would make it a true test! He was willing to sacrifice his child in the same manner as the one who sacrificed their children to Molech. What a vile and disgusting form of morality we see here! A god who wanted to fuck with the mind of a poor peasant. What was going on in Abrahams' head? What did he contemplate as he placed the dagger squarely upon the neck of his son? Are these the feelings that an omnipotent being would like its subjects to feel? Ignore the fact that God stopped Abraham from dealing the final incision to his son's life. All this amounts to is an insecure being that plays mind games with lives that are tantamount to insects. He is a man who spreads salt over slugs for fun. He is a child who enjoys burning ants with a magnifying glass. He required animal sacrifices until only recently, before his own son's death. God is not above a human sacrifice, so Abraham had plenty to be afraid of with regards to the proposed sacrifice of his only son. It is clearly stated in the bible that God can deliver evil upon someone. God is not all good. *"Now the Spirit of the LORD had departed from Saul, and an evil spirit from the LORD tormented him."* - 1 Samuel 16:14. *"I form the light, and create darkness: I make peace, and create evil: I the LORD do all these things."* – Isaiah 45:7.

In another story from the book of morality, Jephthah makes the ultimate sacrifice to Yahweh. *"And Jephthah made a vow to the Lord: 'If you give the Ammonites into my hands, whatever* comes out of the door of my house to meet me when I return in triumph from the Ammonites will be the Lord's, and I will sacrifice it as a burnt offering.' Then Jephthah went over to fight the Ammonites, and the Lord gave them into his hands. He devastated twenty towns from Aroer to the vicinity of Minnith, as far as Abel Keramim. Thus Israel subdued Ammon. When Jephthah returned to his home in Mizpah, who should come out to meet him but his daughter, dancing to the sound of timbrels! She was an only child. Except for her he had neither son nor daughter. When he saw her, he tore his clothes and cried, "Oh no, my daughter! You have brought me down and I am devastated. I have made a vow to the Lord that I cannot break.' 'My father,' she replied, 'you have given your word to the Lord. Do to me just as you promised, now that the Lord has avenged you of your enemies, the Ammonites. But grant me this one request,' she said. 'Give me two months to roam the hills and weep with my friends, because I will never marry.' 'You may go,' he said. And he let her go for two months. She and her friends went into the hills and wept because she would never marry. After the two months, she returned to her father, and he did to her as he had vowed. And she was a virgin. From this comes the Israelite tradition; That the daughters of Israel went yearly to lament the daughter of Jephthah the Gileadite four days in a year." - Judges 11:30-39.

insest ?

Did Yahweh stop Jephthah from committing this dire act of murder? Nowhere in the bible does God absolve Jephthah's oath and tenderly reciprocates by asking for an alternate sacrifice. No, Jehovah allows this unwarranted killing to continue. He allowed this sin. Either way, he is a participant in this death since he is indeed omnipotent. Nowhere does the Bible conclude that God was disgusted with his pledge to him. A loving creator would have thought about the daughter as well.

What about the sacrifice of Jesus? The only way stated in the bible for the creator of everything to forgive humanity was via sacrifice by sending down his son (or himself down, depending on your religious dialect) and have him tortured, humiliated, killed and then raised from the dead? Why does this pass as wisdom? Jesus acted as nothing more than a universal scapegoat. Does this farce pass for intellectual primacy? What did his temporary death accomplish? Did the death of Jesus release a sin erasing mist that propagated and inoculated all human beings from past errors? Did his death appropriate past crimes and blotted out all offenses via a physical manner? No! His death was a symbol for the sacrifice that was needed (in Gods eyes) to balance the broken scales of Jehovah's inept justice. However, the crucifixion of the so-called Christian Messiah is much worse than one could anticipate.

It is my fundamental understanding and a fact that Jesus did not fulfill any of the prophecies listed in the old testament because he is not a descendant of King David or Adam for that matter. Jesus was placed in utero into Mary's body, her ovum fertilized by Gods holy spirit. However, for this to have been true, Jesus would have been born imperfect because he shared DNA with Mary. Also, if Jesus was alive before coming down to heaven, modifying the compilation of his very being would have changed him and would have made him every bit of Mary's son as well. This validates the predominant view in Christianity that Mary is the Mother of God. For Jesus to have been born from Mary, being fully perfect, Mary would have had to have been used solely as a surrogate. No DNA could have contributed to the creation of Jesus. If this is the case, then Jesus was not a descendant of David or Adam and therefore could not have been the promised Messiah. This contradiction makes the following fact obvious. The old testament never indicated that Jesus was to have supernatural origins. The Jews never believed this. They are still waiting for their "human" messiah. The books of Matthew and Luke list a genealogical lineage, albeit a contradictory one but this has no relevance with the proclamation of Jesus as the Messiah since he was not made from any human genetic material. This was a later Christian adaptation that does not allow the two halves of the Christian bible to convolve fully. It becomes apparent that God has screwed humanity in more ways than one.

Let's push the idea of sacrifice to the chasm of human history by moving further in time to the story of Paul. *"Meanwhile, Saul was still breathing out murderous threats against the Lord's disciples. He went to the high priest and asked him for letters to the synagogues in Damascus, so that if he found any there who belonged to the Way (the Christian religion), whether men or women, he might take them as prisoners to Jerusalem. As he neared Damascus on his journey, suddenly a light from heaven flashed around him. He fell to the ground and heard a voice say to him, "Saul, Saul, why do you persecute me?"*

"Who are you, Lord?" Saul asked.

"I am Jesus, whom you are persecuting," he replied. "Now get up and go into the city, and you will be told what you must do."

The men traveling with Saul stood there speechless; they heard the sound but did not see anyone. Saul got up from the ground, but when he opened his eyes, he could see nothing. So they led him by the hand into Damascus. For three days he was blind and did not eat or drink anything.

Logic As Medicine - Morality

In Damascus there was a disciple named Ananias. The Lord called to him in a vision, "Ananias!"

"Yes, Lord," he answered.

The Lord told him, "Go to the house of Judas on Straight Street and ask for a man from Tarsus named Saul, for he is praying. In a vision he has seen a man named Ananias come and place his hands on him to restore his sight."

"Lord," Ananias answered, "I have heard many reports about this man and all the harm he has done to your holy people in Jerusalem. And he has come here with authority from the chief priests to arrest all who call on your name."

But the Lord said to Ananias, "Go! This man is my chosen instrument to proclaim my name to the Gentiles and their kings and to the people of Israel. [16] I will show him how much he must suffer for my name."

Then Ananias went to the house and entered it. Placing his hands on Saul, he said, "Brother Saul, the Lord—Jesus, who appeared to you on the road as you were coming here—has sent me so that you may see again and be filled with the ˙ Holy Spirit." Immediately, something like scales fell from Saul's eyes, and he could see again. He got up and was baptized and after taking some food, he regained his strength.- Acts 9:1-18.

Is it moral that a murderer or conspirator, being intervened by God can now be a preacher of the good news? The most important question to ask is whether or not Paul would have converted if God did *not* intercede? What type of person would Saul (he converted his name to Paul) become if not for his glorious and generous Pauline conversion! If this interaction is moral, are we not *allowed* this same intervention, an intercession that would convert even the most hardened of people? Do not all human beings deserve a religious conversion of this majestic magnitude? If true, it is of utmost importance because as per the book of Revelation, our lives depend on knowing the true religious faith when the end of times arrives.

Christians relish in their genocidal ending, thoughtfully named Armageddon. What the people want is a swift slaughter to anyone that runs in contrast to their beliefs. They are in essence hoping for murder. Death would lead them to the promised land in a similar manner than Muslims who will meet their "Houri" or virgin companions in paradise. It is the pinnacle of achievement, and this can only occur after Gods great slaughter. However, what would happen to us once we are relegated to the realm up above?

Can we live without sadness? The bible tells us we can whether in heaven or an early paradise. However, take that idea and bring it to the real world. Your son just died. You feel great emotional pain. But God can eliminate the pain with the wave of a wand. Would you want to stop grieving the very moment he died? Well, according to the Bible this is exactly what awaits us when we pass. If you die and pass and Armageddon comes and takes the life of your son because he didn't live up to the standards of God or he refused to practice the "truth," what would happen? When you pass and ask where your son is, and you are told he was not worthy, God would make it ok, so you would not grieve. More than that, he would probably erase his mental existence from your mind so that you would not grieve, a spiritual lobotomy of sorts. How disgusting of an idea is this! Is this moral? Is this the best God could conceive as payment for our adoration?

With regards to who enters the gates of heaven, is it moral for a supreme being to reallocate all of its celestial powers for a specific purpose, namely to cajole one single tribe of human society to serve him or her, while depriving the other extant primitive nation states, permitting them to suffer its wrath or deprivation of its security?

We have gone over examples found in the bible which have true currency for these moralistic arguments. I would now like to try a thought experiment with you. I want you to picture your child, boy or girl, vividly in your mind. If you do not have any children, I want you to create one, girl or boy. This generated child should be approximately between 5 – 13 years of age. You should feel true connectedness with this real or fictitious child. If this person were to be affected negatively in any way and you could watch this instance occur, you would surely empathize with this individual. I now want you to close your eyes and watch as this child is molested. You can't even bring yourself to trying to create this simulation! Now, understand that for every 8 minutes, a victim of sexual assault is a child. Now please contemplate on the following scripture. *"The eyes of the LORD are everywhere, keeping watch on the wicked and the good."* – Proverbs 15:3. Is God truly the measuring stick of morality that we all should ascribe to?

We have a great challenge set before us. We need for people to absolve themselves from the morality as denoted in works such as the Bible. We should also be wary of religious parishioners that would like to foist their beliefs on others. They may mean well, but they will look to exalt their form of morality, which we have proven to be false. You never know who the wolves are until they show you their teeth and by that time, it is too late.

Chapter Six

Science is not only a disciple of reason but,
also, one of romance and passion.
- Stephen Hawking

In the previous chapter, I opened up with a passage from the Book of Mathew which I will again cite.

"When they came toward the crowd, a man approached him, knelt down to him, and said: 'Lord, have mercy on my son, because he is an epileptic and is ill. He falls often into the fire and often into the water. I brought him to your disciples, but they could not cure him.' In reply Jesus said: 'O faithless and twisted generation, how long must I continue with you? How long must I put up with you? Bring him here to me.' Then Jesus rebuked the demon, and it came out of him, and the boy was cured from that hour." - Matthew 17:14–18.

When Jesus (God), the originator of the cosmos and creator of all life, specifically human beings, was confronted with an epileptic individual, did he cure his neurological illness by touching his head and somehow halting the incessant random impulses in the brain with his magical powers? No. He exorcized the demon that was controlling this individual's body. Epilepsy is the misfiring of neurons that unconsciously promotes sudden and awkward movements entirely out of the control of the afflicted individual. Demonic exorcism is not a valid form of treatment. If this is the God who created us in whole, why was he ill prepared to administer the proper care? Doctors today can explain in great detail what exactly happens during a seizure. Why is it that human beings (created by God) are better equipped to care for this malady? If Jesus was the creator of all humanity, why did he provide false information to be inscribed in his inspired word?

2 Timothy 3:16 states *"All Scripture is God-breathed (inspired) and is useful for teaching, rebuking, correcting (setting things straight) and training in righteousness,."* What is the lesson of the aforementioned story? Trust in the Lord, and you shall be rewarded with faulty information by God himself? How many times has there been a story in the bible that contradicts with science in even its most elemental understanding? In the bible, it is quite difficult to find a story that convolves perfectly with empirical evidence. The creation myth in the book of Genesis is a perfect example.

What is an evening? What is a morning? An evening can be described as the time when our Sun looks like it is approaching our earthly horizon at the end of the day until it disappears at its datum. A morning is an inversion of this process. It becomes interesting in describing these two basic concepts when considering the creation account in Genesis. *"And God said, "Let there be light," and there was light. God saw that the light was good, and he separated the light from the darkness. God called the light "day," and the darkness he called "night." And there was evening, and there was morning—the first day."* - Genesis 1:3-5. However, even though God created a distinction between light and dark, as a human would do so that they can state that a day occurred, there is no Sun at this point. It is not until the *fourth* day that the great luminaries, the Sun and the Moon are truly created. *"God made two great lights—the greater light to govern the day and the lesser light to govern the night. He also made the stars. God set them in the vault of the sky to give light on the earth, to govern the day and the night, and to separate light from darkness. And God saw that it was good. And there was evening, and there was morning—the fourth day."* - Genesis 1:16-19. It is interesting to note that vegetation was created on the *third* day *before* the Sun was created! *"Then God said, "Let the land produce vegetation: seed-bearing plants and trees on the land that bear fruit with seed in it, according to their various kinds." And it was so. The land produced vegetation: plants bearing seed according to their kinds and trees bearing fruit with seed in it according to their kinds. And God saw that it was good. And there was evening, and there was morning—the third day."* - Genesis 1:11-13. I am trying to marshal my emotions to the best of my capabilities, always leaving open the window of skepticism from both directions, but how on earth was photosynthesis sustainable in plants when there was no Sun? What was the light that was created on the first day? A sophisticated theologian could postulate that the original light was the sudden effects of the big bang, the big flash or explosion, but they would be wrong, not only because the Big Bang created, in essence, a soup of hot particles, but the plasma itself would render the universe opaque, meaning no light could shine through! Not only that but after the plasma cooled down and space became transparent, allowing light to permeate, the early universe then entered what is now known as the dark ages, a period before the first sources of light would start to form. No, the convoluted narrative by the theologian is irreconcilable with the natural observations of the world we live in. Furthermore, The Bible states that the stars were created on the *fourth* day, and stars are the progenitors of light in the cosmos. To prove that the holy word of God is wrong, in the first chapter of the first book no less, renders the rest of its writing inert. I hope that this analysis of the very first words written in the bible renders your pious beliefs inert as well.

Before we move on, let us dissect the fourth day once again. God created the Sun and the stars on the fourth day, at around the same time. This makes sense since the Sun is an actual star, its uniqueness only contrived because it is the center of our solar system. However, how are solar systems created? In an abbreviated summation, a dying star goes supernova. Its contents spill across the cosmos, and a shockwave hurls towards a nearby cloud of dust and gas. The shockwave creates a disturbance in the cloud, which transforms the cloud into a protoplanetary disk and then matter begins to bind with one another via accidental impact. Once a certain mass is achieved, gravity takes over. The gravitational forces attract additional matter up to the point that accretion occurs. The coagulated mass heats up due to the intense pressure created by the gravity of the mass and liquefies. After all of the surrounding matter is obtained, the outer shell of the body can now cool. We now have a rocky planet. Evidence of this accretion process is all around us. When there is a split fissure on earth or a volcano erupts, it spews out liquid magma which is liquid rock and metal. We have all learned in middle school that the earth is comprised of a solid core, a liquid mantle, and a thin solid crust, exactly what you would expect from a planet that had undergone the accretion process.

The question now remains, if this is in fact how planets are created, how was the earth and the heavens (a void in space because there are no stars at this time) created on the first day? "In the beginning, God created the heavens and the earth." - Genesis 1:1. The sun has yet to be created, so how was the earth conceived? The only way to harmonize this wretched abomination of celestial stupidity is that God just waved his magic wand and created the earth. However, this mode of thinking produces its own distinct set of issues. If you are God and you would like to create an object, there would be no limitations or processes to follow. It could create the earth in any way or means he or she preferred. No liquid mantle, no tectonic plates, just a ball of rock for his future creations to inhabit. However, the earth as it currently stands is constructed exactly in the aforementioned manner, by means of a dying star going supernova and the subsequent effects of that cosmic explosion. Did God magically create the earth in a manner to fool humanity into thinking that it was created via natural means? What would be the purpose of this deception? Why would God, unbounded by any laws or restrictions, create the earth in the manner that we observe today? Either God has been operating since the beginning of time disingenuously or, by using the logic principle of Occam's razor, God does not exist.

We are not done, however, with this biblically anatomical examination. As the bible explicitly states in Genesis 1:20-28, he dictates to every animal in the seas, flying creatures, creeping animals and Adam and Eve themselves to *"Be fruitful and become many."* This declaration is not only for the first human pair, as it is typically bequeathed to because this phrase is said twice. The first time is on the fifth day. *"And God said, "Let the water teem with living creatures, and let birds fly above the earth across the vault of the sky." So, God created the great creatures of the sea and every living thing with which the water teems and that moves about in it, according to their kinds, and every winged bird according to its kind. And God saw that it was good. God blessed them and said, "Be fruitful and increase in number and fill the water in the seas, and let the birds increase on the earth." And there was evening, and there was morning—the fifth day."* - Genesis 1:20-23. Humans are made on the sixth day, when this pronouncement is made once again. What is the point to this trivial matter of repetition? The gravity of the proclamation becomes self-evident when looking at the fossil record. It is an absolute fact that approximately over 99% of all species that have ever lived on earth are now extinct. There have been a recorded 5 mass extinctions. In each of these mass extinctions, life in its current state almost ceased to exist. How can this be reconciled with Yahweh's commandment to "be fruitful and become many"? And was this call to action not given to the dinosaurs? How about the mighty Gorgonops, Dimetrodon, Entelodont, Anomalocaris, Dunkleosteus or Postosuchus? How about the non-predatory and plentiful Trilobite, Cynodont or Indricotherium? Were they not to *"be fruitful and become many"?* All of these creatures were created on the fifth and sixth days, so they were indeed given this proclamation. All of the previously listed animals lived before the time of humans so extinction via human means must be ruled out. Also, God provided every obstruction, bombardment or hindrance possible so that they could not complete their task. As the fossil record shows, they were set up for failure, time and time again. Providing an innate compulsion to perform an unachievable task is by definition evil.

As a final nail in the coffin of the creation account, let us examine a definitive hole in the creation mythos on day five. On this day, birds are created, alongside the animals in the seas. On day six, land animals are created. However, again in using the fossil record, we find a glaring hole in this account. Birds are direct descendants of dinosaurs. Fossil evidence establishes that dinosaurs and birds had congruent features such as hollow, pneumatized bones, were nest-builders and had similar digestive behaviors. Archaeopteryx is a classic example of a fossil that fills a missing link gap. This brings us to our inevitable dilemma. Land animals are clearly created on the sixth day, *after* birds! This runs in direct opposition to what Paleontology has shown us! We can even ignore the overwhelming evidence for evolution because the bible does not subscribe to this fact. Let us examine the fossil record. Fossils in lower layers died longer ago than specimens found in higher layers. It can be viewed as the earth tree rings. When do you ever find a bird fossil at a portion of the earth's strata lower than the first land animals? Never! It never happens! Therefore, you can exclude all of the overwhelming evidence that science has culled together, such as similar bodily characteristics, habits, conclusive DNA evidence (it is scientifically proven that a T-Rex and bird are a closer match DNA-wise than an alligator, a reptile) and the fact that feathers developed in the fossil record with dinosaurs and no other such animal. The layers of the stratum show that the land animals came first and that birds came after. There is no way to provide confluence to the text. It is irreconcilable. If God cannot be trusted in showing how he created all living things, in a book that he claims he inspired to write, he cannot be trusted at all. *"Because what may be known about God is clearly evident among them, for God made it clear to them. For his invisible qualities are clearly seen from the world's creation onward, because they are perceived by the things made, even his eternal power and Godship, so that they are inexcusable."* - Roman 1:19-20. Yes. His invisible qualities are clearly on display in the Genesis creation account. Lies, deceit, and fraud.

To further build upon this contradiction, why did God create animals in the manner he did in the first place? What was the purpose? The creation account discusses the abiogenesis of all living things on earth, especially animals. If the Bible indicates with absolute certainty that *"through sin, death entered the world,"* why did God create certain animals with specific features not needed in the Garden of Eden?

For example, if I were to ask a person to cut a single piece of paper and presented two instruments to achieve this task, a pair of scissors and a chainsaw; this person would undoubtedly choose the scissors. If you had asked this person, why they made their selection, they would state that the scissors were the right tool for the job. However, both instruments would cut the paper. A chainsaw would cut the paper with ease. So, why does a person not use a chainsaw to cut a piece of paper?

There are some hindrances when using a chainsaw to cut paper. You would need fuel to cut the paper when scissors only require kinetic energy from your hand. A chainsaw will create a sloppy cut when a pair of scissors are extremely precise, although they both can perform the task.

If we study the anatomy of a chainsaw, we can deduce quite quickly that the intent of this device is not to cut paper. You could hypothesize that it was designed with the purpose to cut dense wood pulp, in the form of live wood trees. How can we ascertain this design intent? We can study the teeth of the chain. The multitude of continuous sharp edges would be perfect for continuous removal of wood from a tree trunk or branch. The gas or electric powered motor provides the adequate horsepower to drive the various blades into the tree trunk with ease. Looking at the characteristics of the chainsaw would provide clues into the purpose of its creation.

Let us for the time being delude ourselves temporarily and state that God created all living beings. Why did God create dinosaurs, the venerable Tyrannosaurus Rex for example? Many fundamentalists will undoubtedly declare that God had a purpose and when that purpose was fulfilled, he removed them from this earth. I will not argue with this sly deployment of apologetic verbiage. We can use another animal that lived in the Garden of Eden as a perfect alternative example.

The Garden of Eden is the fictional place that is described in the book of Genesis. It is fictional because the evidence shows that the Y-chromosome Adam and the mitochondrial Eve lived more than 100,000 years ago and not approximately 6,000 years ago as calculated by using the Bible. The evidence also shows that the original progenitors were not the only members of the homo genus alive at the time. However, speaking from a purely Biblical standpoint, let us mentally provide yet again another concession and state that Eden was real and that the biblical Adam and Eve existed.

According to ancient lore, the Garden of Eden was a vast forest that Yahweh created that would soon house every living thing that we see today, including the first human pair. It also included all domesticated animals. That biblical fact is so odiously incorrect that we will not venture far into that territory. Domesticated animals are creatures that were tamed by humans themselves and using artificial selection; they became a different species of animal. This is well documented and not up for questioning. God did not create dogs, cows, and pigs. Cows, for example, were created approximately 10,000 years ago, before the advent of the Judeo-Christian God. That aside, Eden was supposed to be the culmination of perfect creation, starting with the cosmos and completed with the creation of man and woman. A perfect world where death had no dominion over.

If this is the case, why did God create lions? Like the chainsaw, we can discern the reason for its invention. Look at its teeth. Its dental composition is typical of carnivores. Admire the dense muscle secured to its appendages. Study its claws. Realize that this creature, if created, was created as a killing machine. The "Fall," the instance where sin propagated into the world did not morph a previously banal feline into a murderer. The tombstones of the fossil record do not substantiate this thinking. No, God created these hunters and therefore created death, if you ascribe to intelligent design, which we are for the sake of this argument. What about the cobra, the black widow spider or the alligator? Why would God construct these killers in a perfect paradise? Why bestow these carnivorous killing machines with teeth made for shredding meat or inducing venom but have them eat grain? *"And to all the beasts of the earth and all the birds in the sky and all the creatures that move along the ground--everything that has the breath of life in it--I give every green plant for food." And it was so.* – Genesis 1:30. How is this viewed as intelligent design? Who would consider the man that cuts the single piece of paper with a chainsaw instead of with scissors intelligent? Why should we then view the entity who created a lion in the Garden of Eden intelligent as well?

It should be hopefully obvious that God did not create the lion and that all of the felines of today were created via the mechanism of natural selection. The evidence of evolution is overwhelming, and yet people still have a difficult time coming to terms with this invisible shaper of life. The sinister mirage of evolution is that in the absence of contemporary knowledge, life itself is the perfect showcase for an intelligent designer. It is only when you look deeper and without the use of confirmation bias that the truth is revealed.

The recurrent laryngeal nerve is a classic example of intelligent design gone wrong. I am not the first person to point out this design flaw, but I feel that it has not been adequately disseminated for all to hear. The laryngeal nerve supplies the brain signals to muscles that manipulate the vocal cords housed in the larynx. Without these signals, we would not be able to talk, amongst other things. We can think of the various parts in this manner; the laryngeal nerve is our biological speaker wire, the larynx is the speaker, and the brain is our audio receiver which sends out auditory signals to the speakers.

The problem with an intelligent designer becomes self-evident when looking at the placement of the laryngeal nerve in various animals. The laryngeal nerve (bundled in the vagus nerve and then branches out) travels from the brain, down the neck, then wraps around the great vessels coming out of the heart, makes a u-turn and then travels up the neck again where it connects to the larynx. Why does it take this route when a more direct path is possible? This occurs because of evolution via natural selection. Our ancestors, early fish, used this same path of travel but fish do not have necks, so the design flaw was minimized. As we evolved into mammals, we developed necks, and the error in the path of the laryngeal nerve was magnified. This gross mistake in engineering is most easily seen in the path of the laryngeal nerve in a giraffe. There is a great video with Professor Richard Dawkins on National Geographic's "Inside Nature's Giants," which I recommend everyone to watch, in which an autopsy is performed on a giraffes neck, and the path of the laryngeal nerve is followed. It uses the same path found in humans and fish, but because of its unusually long neck, this particular nerve is approximately 15 feet long when the distance from the brain to the larynx is only 2 inches away! How can we consider this to be intelligently designed?

The wiring of a home theater media room perfectly explains the aforementioned conundrum we previously observed. Imagine that you are sitting on the sofa watching your favorite movie. The wall speakers and audio receiver are on the same wall and are only feet apart from each other. The media wall will represent our giraffe head. As an intelligent AV installer, he or she would naturally connect the two pieces of equipment directly, while hiding the wires in the wall, for aesthetic purposes. The only problem is that this installer was not intelligent. This installer's chosen wiring path was to go from the receiver, out of the room to the family room, past the family room, and down the stairs, through the laundry room and into the boiler room. The installer would then wrap the wire around one of the water pipes from the boiler and then proceed out the boiler room, through the laundry room, up the stairs, through the family room, back into the media room and then connect the wiring to the wall speakers.

Science As Medicine - Facts

If we solicited the services of a capable A/V installer, which one of us would allow this installation to occur? Which one of us would *pay* for this appalling installation? No one would. We would immediately question the installers experience and skill set. If we will not tolerate the stupidity of this hypothetical human installer, why would we grant the title of intelligent designer to the deity that created all things? If an intelligent designer created all animals from scratch, this progressive deterioration of engineering would never have happened. The reason for this design flaw? Natural selection, a non-intelligent driving force, cannot go back to the drawing board. An intelligent creator, however, could have, but as we can see from the fossil record, it never did. God did not create all living things. The bodies of all living things were molded like clay via natural selection.

If God created all animals and more specifically humans, then there would be no biologically trackable relationships between them. Well, there could be shared characteristics, if God was lazy with his creation and lacked imagination. If you are an omnipotent being with a limitless range of creative potential, there should be no extent to its creation. A human's function is very different from a fish or a giraffe. If an intelligent designer created human beings to serve him and not to be part of the animal kingdom, then the anatomy of a human would be significantly different. That is not what we see in the structure of arms in all mammalian vertebrates.

If we look at the structure of a human arm, we see a pattern of bones found in all vertebrates and also with one of our earliest known ancestors, Tiktaalik. The human arm is comprised of the Humerus; the bone that runs from the shoulder to the elbow, the Radius and the Ulma; the two bones that run from the elbow to the wrist and the Carpal, which are our wrist bones and the bones that comprise our fingers. This bone structure is found in bats, birds, frogs, cats, whales, horses, giraffes and Tiktaalik, the first commonly known primitive fish/tetrapod predecessor that walked on land and is the hypothesized precursor to all vertebrate land animals.

Why is this a problem? If an intelligent designer went back to the drawing board when creating humans, there would be no need for two bones to travel from the elbow to the wrist. This design flaw makes humans susceptible to forearm fractures, one of the most common fractures. This injury occurs when a person falls and outstretches their arms to dampen the fall. A proper forearm structural support could be comprised of one single large bone as thick as the aforementioned Humerus which could handle the trauma above.

Speaking of intelligent design, what about the design of the human being itself? Intelligence has a limit, much like a cup of tea. It can be filled to the brim but pass that, and it will spill its contents onto the table. It can only hold so much. You cannot make the cup larger, so you are stuck with that capacity. You are born with this "cup."

The brain is composed of approximately 100 billion neurons but weighs only 3 pounds. A lot is crammed into this small organ. Your entire ability to emerge into consciousness stems from the matter that is compressed within the confines of your skull. Everything that makes you who you are, minus your interactions with reality is comprised of that very organ.

Earlier I stated, "You are born with this cup." That is not entirely accurate. You were created with that cup, your cranium, if you ascribe to intelligent design. The extremities of your skull are the limits of your mind. The intelligence you have does in a way correspond with your skulls volumetric capacity. Therefore, your cranium is in effect limiting your intellectual potential. Your body mass to brain matter ratio has been maximized. Nevertheless, is it the skull that is limiting you?

How are we born? Our mothers push us out through the birth canal, and there, we find our true limit. It is the cervix. If we were able to evolve larger brains, we would in effect cause great damage to the progenitor's vagina. Already, episiotomies are done to enlarge the birth "opening" when necessary. If we evolved even larger heads, this could lead to a painful outcome for the maternal progenitor; a possibly fatal result. Since this death of both the child and mother would not progress the evolutionary metronome, this potential positive evolvement of our brains is not possible. In essence, we can blame God's engineering of the vagina for our ignorance, insofar as to why we are not even smarter; why our minds have reached our maximum potential. Another flaw found in the design of Gods cherished creation.

While on the subject, let's discuss episiotomies, cesarean sections and other difficulties in childbirth. Child labor is still one of the deadliest things that a woman can go through. Childbirth is currently the sixth most common cause of death among women between the ages of 20 and 34 in the United States. That being said, imagine how many individuals died during child labor *before* the time of modern medicine, without the aid of current knowledge and advanced medical technology? If an assembly line broke down and therefore failed to produce a finished product, such as a car in that frequency, we would have to question the design of the assembly line outlined by its designer. In the same vein, if a human being could not be created without fear of death, we need to ascertain if the design of the human assembly line is well thought out. Is this another engineering defect overlooked by the architect of our creation?

Before this assembly line of humanity was instituted, Yahweh created the first woman, Eve, from the rib of Adam. This account, found in Genesis 2:22, along with many scriptures in the old testament and the various utterances purportedly spoken by the apostle Paul, have acted as the principal lynchpins of the calculated subjugation of women throughout the ages. If these verses are taken to be true, then the creator of our species has an interesting sense of humor. If God created Adam first and Eve was created from Adam, why is it that in utero, we all start as women? If the fetus is to be a boy, it is not until later that the y chromosome is expressed and that the required changes to its body are made. However, by this time the nipples and mammary glands required for the female body have already been created. This is why gynecomastia is possible in males. If an excess of estrogen is present, the existing female mammary glands will further develop, similar to what happens in a females puberty phase and it is quite possible that a male with this condition can lactate!

What about scientific blunders that reach beyond our celestial homeland? On Monday, August the 21st 2017, a total solar eclipse was viewed by millions in 14 states in the United States, spanning from Oregon to South Carolina. All looked up in anticipation to see one of the random marvels bestowed by our solar system. Many read in advance the newspaper articles in which scientists explained the science behind the event so they could appreciate the eclipse even more, by understanding the underpinnings of this celestial phenomenon. The comprehension of the mechanics of its majesty does nothing to hinder its unequivocal beauty, as the mask made by our nighttime luminary is temporarily placed upon its brighter counterpart. However, what if this heavenly event occurred much earlier, before our knowledge of modern astronomy?

"I will show wonders in the heavens above and signs on the earth below, blood and fire and billows of smoke. The sun will be turned to darkness and the moon to blood before the coming of the great and glorious day of the Lord. And everyone who calls on the name of the Lord will be saved." Acts 2:19-21

As per the scripture above, the darkening of the Sun portends 'the glorious day of God.' The science of a solar eclipse was not yet known at that time, so in this verse, it is attributed to the end of days, naturally. What about the description of the moon turning to blood? It is typical for the moon to become a shade of red during a lunar eclipse. This occurs due to the sunlight entering the earth's atmosphere, filtering out the high energy wavelengths of the light spectrum (violet, blue, green, etc) but allowing the low energy wavelengths, predominantly the red portion of the visible spectrum, to pass through and illuminate the moon, giving the moon its reddish quality. So, in essence, the writer of this scripture takes two standard astronomical occurrences and convolves the two, all while injecting their perceived reasoning behind these events, the last days before the second coming of the Messiah. Call upon the name of the Lord, and you will be saved.

Let us fast-forward to today. Seeing the light snatched by the Sun and the Moon cast with a blood-like hue would not incite panic to the majority of the knowledgeable public in our time. A fog of hysteria would solely be relegated to people in times past, before the proliferation of contemporary understanding. The authors of the Bible lacked these basic fundamentals so they drew their own conclusions via their intuition, which always had tints of sin, shadows of calamity, shades of redemption and broad brush strokes of forgiveness and everlasting life; an unverifiable hope used as a source of comfort, a psychological border drawn with bold lines on our minds canvas created to protect us from this cruel world.

A perfect example of this intuition in action is the winter solstice. As the days approached the winter solstice, the travel "arc path" of the sun (the sun was worshipped as a God at this time) dropped lower and lower in the sky. People were concerned that this direction of movement would continue until the sun would never appear! During the winter solstice, however, it appeared that the sun halted its decent. This is why the solstice (the Middle English word derived from the Latin word sol and stit, mean 'sun stopped') was worshiped. After the solstice, the sun began its ascension once again and paved the way for the future harvest and warmer temperatures.

The people of that time provided in their minds a perfectly lucid explanation to what they observed. It was however entirely inaccurate. The winter solstice only occurs because of the earth's tilt. It is merely a function of Non-Euclidean geometry, a side effect of living on a tilted oblate spheroid traveling around a relatively fixed light source. This celestial phenomenon is no more special than the aforementioned solar and lunar eclipse; it's perceived importance only housed within the mind of the archaic human being of yore.

This self-imposed attached rider to reality is how mythology began. Mankind endeavors to explain the to and fro's of our worlds mechanics, the explanations to the celestial movements;   it's mechanisms hidden behind the veiled blue curtain of the sky.

Science is a thought method which allows us to separate factual conclusions from the illusion of our intuition. Our perception of the world is blanketed in our own biases and cultural experiences. No one can truly say that their cognitive abilities have never been affected by the bouquet of emotions, stimuli, and experiences of our world. The scientific method attempts to sanitize us of our own intuitive leanings. A great example of our intuitions failing is the answer to the following question.

A bat and ball cost $1.10. The bat costs one dollar more than the ball. How much does the ball cost? The overwhelming majority of people got this wrong, including students from prestigious schools. Why? Because humans put great faith in their innate intuitions. If this problem can easily make people slip up, how can we trust our intuitions when it comes to God?

This is why the scientific method was invented. It allows us to decouple intuition and reality to determine what is true in this world, whereas religion is a pseudo-scientific field led by people ignorant of observation and experimentation, which pontificates doctrine as physical law. This is a method that did not exist in the prior biblical Bronze age. If so, the errors found in the bible would have been reduced greatly. This is evidence in itself that God did not inspire the Bible. Ostensibly, God can inspire others to write his word, but he has no editorial capabilities. How powerful could this version of God be?

Chapter Seven

Science and technology revolutionize our lives, but memory,
tradition and myth frame our response.
- Arthur M. Schlesinger

Some people believe that crushed rhino horn can cure a range
of illnesses and it is even viewed as an aphrodisiac in Traditional
Asian Medicine. However, the rhino horn is comprised of keratin,
the same material as our fingernails and has no medicinal value. If
rhino horn proved to have medicinal benefits, it would mean that
we too can acquire these effects by biting our fingernails!
Unfortunately, this ill-conceived notion is the reason why rhinos
are being hunted to extinction. Look at what belief can make
people do.

Vaccines are the most effective and practical method of
preventing diseases. The science that supports this method of
illness prevention is solid. Vaccinations have been responsible for
the elimination of measles, polio, and smallpox. However, even

though science has not shown any correlation whatsoever, many parents insist on believing that vaccines can lead to autism. This has led to many parents withholding important vaccinations from their children. I have personally seen the damage done to children and adults who were not vaccinated. I have seen people crippled by illnesses that could have easily been avoided by vaccinations. Look at what belief can make a parent do.

For strictly observant Orthodox Jews on Fridays, sundown ushers in the observance of Shabbat, the Jewish Sabbath. Since it is forbidden to use or adjust electric switches or to kindle (create) a fire, wood burning, gas or otherwise, hundreds of thousands of observant Jews leave their Sabbath candles and hot plates on and unattended from Friday night to Saturday night, even when they leave their homes. In 2015 after a malfunctioning hot plate started a fire in a Jewish Brooklyn home that killed seven family members, the Fire Departments safety education unit handed out fire-safety literature to educate the Jewish neighbors on how to observe the Sabbath safely. However, the neighbors could not accept the literature, due to the Sabbath rules. Look at what belief can make an adult do.

When a child is facing death due to an illness, a parent should do anything they need to do to save that child's life. If the child needs a blood transfusion, we should do everything in our power to get that child a blood transfusion. We would look into our health insurance or create a payment plan or at the extreme, mortgage our belongings to help our children. This compulsion to help our children is innate in all of us. However, according to the Jehovah's Witnesses religion, since God has condemned the consumption of blood (Acts 15:29, Genesis 9:4), blood transfusions are not allowed. Adherents to the JW faith must look into other ways their child can be treated and watch them die when a blood transfusion is the only solution to a grand culmination of failed treatments. Look at what belief can make a parent do.

It is assumed that undue stress can kill you. The World Health Organization has called stress the "health epidemic of the 21st century." These claims have led to an even greater need and focus on maintaining a healthy work-life balance. However, a published study in 2012 indicated that high levels of stress *alone* did not increase their risk of dying. However, if high levels of stress were coupled with the *belief* that stress could harm their health, the risk of dying increased by 43%! Look at what belief *alone* can do.

Belief has the uncanny ability to couple fear with consequence and then provide a barrier to understanding based off of the self-imposed doctrine of the faith. A perfect example is a person's fear of flying more than driving on the road since driving is typically a natural occurrence in their lives. However, driving is much more dangerous statistically. Humans in the United States had a 1 in 114 chance of dying in a car crash. On the other hand, Americans had a 1 in 9,821 chance of dying in a plane crash. You rarely hear of a person who has a fear of driving or being in a car that rivals the feverous tempest associated with the fear of flying. Why is this the case? Why is belief such a potent elixir in people's way of thinking? What is the problem with belief?

Belief can only truly take hold in a group, village, society or person in where facts no longer have currency over their convictions. This is perfectly displayed during war. With so much bloodshed, the facts are tangible enough to ascertain that this course of action (if the war is not via a means of protecting oneself) will only produce death and destruction. However, a belief that *"God is on our side"* or *"our race is vastly superior"* can obfuscate the facts and catapult the aggressor to commit heinous acts. The German army in WW2 or the Crusades are perfect examples. Another more benign example can be an incorrect "fact" learned in the past that when corrected, one can feel offended or uncomfortable. My son's teacher taught that the days in summer get longer as time progresses. I explained to her that the summer solstice, the first day of summer, is the longest day of the year. Therefore every superseding day of summer is shorter! Even after providing this objective fact, I could sense the trepidation in her voice. At the end of our conversation, she told me *"Well, I still think that you are wrong. You can have your beliefs, and I can have mine."* This is an utterance from an educator! This is how belief can make a teacher or any other person act. This is the problem with belief.

Belief can also lead a person to attribute beneficial circumstances to a divine being. Religious attribution can fundamentally change a person. When we welcome the birth of a new child or are happy that we landed a new and better-paying position at work or are excited about the purchase of a first home, many people can look back and recollect the hard work that it took for these things to have been fully realized. However, there are a great many deal of people who attribute every beneficial event to one entity. God. *"How did I survive that trying ordeal when I was homeless for months and yet was able to find steady work and finally find a place for rent? It was by the spirit of God that these things occurred and by means of his holy spirit that I was able to endure." "How was I able to combat my drug addiction when it consumed every thought I had? Obviously God had a hand in steering my life's rudder."* As false as this thinking is, what is the harm with these thoughts?

The Problem With Belief

Religious attribution is a parasite that removes parts of our very humanity. It reduces our instinctual drive. It stops the thought or idea that we are the keepers of our lives. It makes one abandon determination, especially if predestination is believed. It inadvertently generates low self-esteem. How? If we attribute everything to God, then we have accomplished nothing in our lives. If we need to rely on someone for everything we do, what good are we? It also sabotages their long-term planning, since they have placed everything in Gods hands. Are you poor and hungry? God will provide. "*Therefore do not be anxious, saying, 'What shall we eat?' or 'What shall we drink?' or 'What shall we wear?' For the Gentiles seek after all these things, and your heavenly Father knows that you need them all.*" – Matthew 6:31-32. "*Which of you, if your son asks for bread, will give him a stone? Or if he asks for a fish, will give him a snake? If you, then, though you are evil, know how to give good gifts to your children, how much more will your Father in heaven give good gifts to those who ask him!*" – Matthew 7:9-11.

What about life and death? If you are only hungry, this may be relatively easy to fix, depending on your own circumstances. However, what if your beliefs lead you to a path where death is imminent? What if you can avoid this end, but you intentionally steer into the danger of knowing that you will not survive? Can belief truly make you commit suicide?

The religion of the Jehovah's Witnesses is a perfect example of how their convictions can override their own survival instincts. Jehovah's Witnesses do not accept blood transfusions of any kind, regardless of the circumstances. They attribute this belief to a scripture in the book of Acts. "*Instead, we should write and tell them to abstain from eating food offered to idols, from sexual immorality, from eating the meat of strangled animals, and from consuming blood."* – Acts 15:20. Their rationality is that blood transfusions did not exist during the time of the apostle Paul and therefore could not have been condemned. The spirit of the verse in their doctrinal prism is that ingesting blood of any kind, even intravenously, would conflict with this inspired utterance. Therein lies the problem. Let us ignore that this is factually incorrect. The two methods of "ingestion" do not lead to the same outcomes. Transfusions will increase the actual blood levels in humans. Eating the blood would digest the blood and provide nutrients to the blood but would not raise blood levels. Their belief in succumbing to the fundamentals taught in an old book overrides logic. Jehovah's Witnesses can say whatever they want about this sentence, but in the real world, parents would let their children die, in the name of belief. Adults would commit suicide by not accepting blood transfusions and would rather die as martyrs than defy their organization's interpretation of scripture.

The problem with Jehovah's Witnesses fervent drive to follow all of the biblical viewpoints with extreme accuracy and without waiver (such as their abstaining from blood transfusions) is not in fundamentalism. It is the actual fundamentals. When the Bible teaches that Abraham was told by God to kill his firstborn son Isaac and Abraham held the knife out to kill his only son, only to have God say that this was a test of his faith and belief in God shows the level of piety that the Bible calls for. *"When they reached the place God had told him about, Abraham built an altar there and arranged the wood on it. He bound his son Isaac and laid him on the altar, on top of the wood. Then he reached out his hand and took the knife to slay his son. But the angel of the LORD called out to him from heaven, "Abraham! Abraham!" "Here I am," he replied. "Do not lay a hand on the boy," he said. "Do not do anything to him.*

The Problem With Belief

Now I know that you fear God because you have not withheld from me your son, your only son." – Genesis 22:9-12. This scripture indicates how strident parishioners should be in their belief in God. This verse should scare anyone who is religious or seeking spirituality in any Abrahamic faith. Belief is so strong that it can make a person perceive this religious story in a good light. *"How faithful was Abraham that he was willing to give his only son as a sacrifice to God!"* It is these fundamentals that fuel the Jehovah's Witnesses beliefs and is what makes them dangerous to themselves, their children and others.

Belief, however, has many facets that are not couched in God and are not specifically spiritual. The belief that the earth is flat is one such concept, and it is growing in America. Something as factual as the understanding of the earth as an oblate spheroid is now a point of contention, incomprehensibly so. There are now Flat Earth societies that spew primordial rhetoric composed of Pre-Pythagorean nonsensical logic. Even worse, these very societies that claim to free one's mind of the lies being told to children at schools and on TV now declare in a parroting manner the 'truth' about the earth and epitomize their adherents to promote these lies in a ventriloquistic manner.

However, as bad as advocating these lies are, the actual devout belief of a flat earth has the side effect of compelling oneself to believe other nonsense that is required to maintain faith in said belief. We have been able to traverse along the complete surface of the earth and yet there are no reports of people falling off the edge. How does a faithful flat earther reconcile reality with their beliefs? According to news reports, the answer is now teleportation! In the same manner as the game Pac-Man, once a person or object such as a plane reaches the edge of the earth, they are teleported to the other side instantaneously and without knowing that it happened! These are the types of fictitious "facts" one must believe to harmonize their flat earth faith with truth. This can even be proven true through a silly, made up story.

I would like to tell you a quick story I heard in my childhood about the beginning of the insect population. The story is about the first insect, Queen Antius. In the beginning, reptiles, mammals & birds were at war with one another for domination over the earth. The birds had flight. The reptiles had their strength, and the mammals had their versatility. The fighting lasted for millennia until a new breed of animal was not created but arrived. It was the creator of all animals; Queen Antius. She had the powers of all of the animals and created the three separate animal dominions in her image. The birds had flight; the wings were variations of hers. The reptiles had her strength but lacked her armored body. The mammals had her versatility, just like her versatility in creation. Queen Antius ushered forth a new breed of animal, giant insects but they were still too weak to fight the other three animal dominions so in a moment of despair, Queen Antuis shrank the insects as punishment for their folly, and she flew above the earth and exploded in a ball of light as a sacrifice to all of the animal dominions, to shock them into understanding the error of their ways. They continue to fight one another as a food source but the time of wanton death was over. High above the sky was left a halo of the Queen's image as a remembrance to all of what occurred. This is the story of Queen Antius.

In 2013 the European Space Agency's Herschel Space Observatory focused its gaze on Menzel 3, a nebula located in the constellation Norma. It is called the Ant Nebula. It is comprised of the ejecting atmosphere of a dying star. However, something is

The Problem With Belief

keeping the material in the same space, which is creating a very dense cloud, approximately 10,000 more dense than usual. The hypothesis is that the ejected material is being attracted by the gravitational force of a neighboring star. This dense neighbor is influencing the shape of the nebula and is creating the Ant Nebulas head and thorax resemblance.

However, if hypothetical "Anters" (people who adhere to the belief of Queen Antuis) were asked about the findings, one could speculate that their response would be of apprehension and then of consilience, as long as their faith was kept intact. They would approach the situation with a qualifier such as *"Well, this is the science behind the explosion generated by Queen Antius. When she gave her life away as a sacrifice for all, her implosion generated two stars, one that represents her mind and one that represents her heart. The Nebula is the "halo" that was described in the books of Antia. We agree with the scientific findings".*

I hope it goes without saying that this story is not true, but it shows what belief can hypothetically make a person think. The cognitive dissonance ingrained in their prefabricated thoughts would not allow them to come to the overarching conclusion that Queen Antuis never existed and that the Ant Nebula is nothing more than a gas cloud shaped in the semblance of an ant. They will also point to the fact that giant insects once roamed the earth and can be found in the fossil record, so this too proves that Queen Antius existed.

This elastic thinking goes for religion as well. To square the real world with religious faith, one must be ready to accept some quite complex absurdities. The Pac-Man paradox works just as well in religious belief. A perfect example is a battle against the Amorites recorded in Joshua chapter 10.

The Problem With Belief

Then Joshua spoke to the LORD *in the day when the* LORD *delivered up the Amorites before the children of Israel, and he said in the sight of Israel:*

"Sun, stand still over Gibeon;
And Moon, in the Valley of Aijalon."
So the sun stood still,
And the moon stopped,
Till the people had revenge
Upon their enemies.

Is this not written in the Book of Jasher? So the sun stood still in the midst of heaven, and did not hasten to go down for about a whole day. And there has been no day like that, before it or after it, that the LORD *heeded the voice of a man; for the* LORD *fought for Israel.* – Joshua 10:12-14.

An interesting story indeed but what would be the consequence of the Sun and the Moon standing still for approximately 12 hours? For this to occur, the earth would need to suddenly stop spinning on its axis. Once this happened, everything that is not attached to the ground would be hurled at a speed of 1,000 miles per hour into space or into another object secured to the ground. The atmosphere would still be rotating at the original speed so it would scrub out of existence the actual topography of the earth. If you were to survive all of this somehow, your barely alive body would have to endure the same conditions all over again as the earth started to rotate.

Is it possible that this story happened? Of course not, but since the bible carries no faults, that has not stopped apologists from flexing the realm of possibility to contour to their beliefs. Many explanations have been given to reconcile this story with reality. It has been said that the entire bible, although inspired by an all-knowing God is written from the perspective of the writer. Apparently God can inspire others to write his word but does not have the ability to proofread the actual work. It has been said that God provided a nonmoving light that was perceived as the sun. It is however also described as literary writing that is an allegory to the actual fighting that ensued and that it describes Gods undying commitment to his people. The fundamental apologists state that if God is all-powerful, then it is within his power to do what the story describes, all while keeping the earth and its inhabitants safe. If God is omnipotent, then nothing is impossible.

Notice the Pac Man paradox at work in these explanations, namely that if one can think of a scenario that satisfies the encapsulated inerrancy of the Bible, then it is possible, regardless if the account does not conform to the rules of reality. God does not need to follow his own self-imposed natural laws because he is the one who creates such rules and is the unmoving mover in this game. This is what belief can make a person envision as a sane thought.

What do these beliefs in an inerrant yet omnipotent being lead to? The outcomes vary by the religion but all share one thing, namely that these old collections of stories should be taken literally and that we should contour our lives and base them off of these very accounts. With Jehovah's Witnesses, there are no blood transfusions, and there's rampant child molestation, because in rape there are not two witnesses of the crime like required in the bible. Clay figurines without faces so as not to be taken as graven images and avoidance of technology since they are no part of this world occur with the Amish. The Catholic Church's injunction that the use of condoms is considered immoral has led to the widespread wildfire of AIDS to spread across the globe. Holy wars were fought in the name of God where countless people were killed. Beheadings and wanton terrorism are handed out in multitude by Muslim extremists. Flat Earthers teach their children to question well-established facts. This is only a small sample of what belief has created. It only scratches beneath the surface. People will follow the rules but choose which rules to follow. Human beings, no matter how brutish they may be, always find a way to color within the lines.

What about religious belief that has no apparent negative consequences? Imagine their mother joins a group of people called the Winners. Their central tenant of belief is that the head of the organization states that all members of the group, as long as they accept and fulfill the doctrines of the organization will receive a $100,000,000.00 winning lottery ticket. The ticket may be given to you tomorrow or 30 years from now, but the ticket is a guaranteed winner. Your mother believes in this idea and models her life around the Winners doctrine, which includes being nice to others, feeding the poor, paying the tithe to the Winners leader and not taking any risks in life, because life is sacred and taking any risks puts your life in danger and can make you a "Loser".

She follows these tenants and although she had dreams of riding a hot air balloon, firing her first gun in a shooting range and flying around the globe to see the world; she puts all of those desires on hold to conform to the Winners life plan. She practices her group's beliefs for many years, and now, she is in bad health. She realizes that she will die before receiving her winning ticket, but part of the doctrine states that if a person were to die before claiming their winnings, the ticket would be passed down to their next of kin or specified recipient. She passes away a few years later. Her son, who did not like her association with this group, nonetheless meets the Winners leader and he is then told, after much persuasion that there never was a winning ticket.

The Problem With Belief

The son goes home to grieve and is consoled by friends and family. The son then explains that the group's leader lied about the winning ticket. His family and friends say "At least she lived a happy life and did well throughout the world. Even if the ticket was a lie, she was a moral and upstanding citizen!"

How is this any consolation? The answer is that it is not. She may have lived a moral life, but she did not live her life to the fullest, the only life she had. She never satisfied her desires to travel the world, ride a hot air balloon or fulfill any of her other dreams. If there is no life after this one, part of having a fulfilled life is to experience all of the great things this life has to offer. This mother was robbed of those moments. These are the consequences of belief.

This example ties perfectly with modern day religion. I have been told that "Even if God is a lie, I would have still lived a moral and good life so what would be the harm in a belief of God?" The answer would be the same as the story above.

Time and time again we see how a belief in something that is factually or ethically incorrect can lead to damaging consequences. However, some of these negative effects occur so far along in the future that the correlation between belief and real-life consequences is not easily visible. The ancient story of the curse of Ham in Genesis 9:20-27 was later used and interpreted to indicate where black skin came from and since this marking was an indication of servitude to the other nations at that time, it was used as justification that Blacks were to be slaves. The fact that it was the Jews that sought to kill the purported Messiah Jesus Christ was used as reasoning for anti-Semitism in the future, and this hatred towards a nation of people was the bedrock for the Holocaust. In the second part of Genesis 3:16 - *"Your desire will be for your husband, and he will rule over you.'*... has been used for millennia in keeping women constrained in positions of being solely a housekeeper, bearer of children and away from positions of power. The women's rights movement would not have been necessary if not for this verse. Homosexuals have been ostracized, killed and otherwise persecuted because of verses in the New Testament.

Is there any hope that these beliefs can be blotted out of existence? Negative ideologies that are erected by factions within society and not by an omnipotent and omniscient being always follow the pendulum of consensus in due time. We can only hope that today's religions follow the same logic, but unwarranted belief is something that humanity will have to deal with for the rest of their existence.

Chapter Eight

People to whom sin is just a matter of words,
to them salvation is just words too.
- William Faulkner

Over the years, religion has justified its existence via passages from a holy book and have stated that since the quotes listed in these writings are inspired by their God, they should be adhered to as fact. Past arguments would involve a quote from scripture as their basis of faith and that these truths were undeniable. These truths included that the world was flat, that the Earth was the center of the solar system or universe, that every creature on the planet was created by God and so on. However, when science provided facts that were contrary to these truths, these principals were either stated to have never been true in the first place or were assimilated into their beliefs. This retroactive evidentialism has continued throughout the history of religion in the face of science. If a sentient creator compelled men to write these books via inspiration and revelation, then why is such fine-tuning of their beliefs essential? I have heard the argument from progressive Christians that the Bible, for example, was written so far back in time that you must understand the Bible in its context and that you cannot bring a modern idea into the classic religious infrastructure without violating or harming scripture. This point of contention falls flat on its face as it places the supreme deity in a position of disenfranchisement, a creator without all of the answers.

The one concept however that almost everyone will concede to is sin. Even the most nonchalant of believers and most non-religious people agree on sin. It has been the most pervasive idea that has porously infiltrated society in general. Sin is on the continuum of a crime, even if the person does not believe in divine law. What's the harm in the interchangeability between using sin and crime? It seems like a trivial distinction until statements like "we are all sinful" or "we are all imperfect" permeate the world's population. It is not the idea that we have committed sins in the past that is radioactive. It is the fact that we have all been *born* sinful that is truly toxic.

The concept that we have all been born into sin is the doctrine of original sin, and this belief is a prerequisite for all Abrahamic faiths. It states that newly born children are innately and automatically evil. It is a disgusting doctrine that says we have all been born defective in our full capacities and that we need extraterrestrial guidance and forgiveness in the form of Gods love, patience and mercy to live life as intended. There are many presuppositions in that statement that are incorrect, but the idea that we need Gods forgiveness is the most sinister. This maxim is rooted in the fallacious myth of human creation. The story of Adam and Eve is the start of this pernicious belief.

It's As Original As Sin

"To Adam, he said, "Because you listened to your wife and ate fruit from the tree about which I commanded you, 'You must not eat from it,'

"Cursed is the ground because of you;
through painful toil, you will eat food from it
all the days of your life.
It will produce thorns and thistles for you,
and you will eat the plants of the field.
By the sweat of your brow
you will eat your food
until you return to the ground,
since from it you were taken;
for dust you are
and to dust you will return." – Genesis 3:17-19

Thus begins original sin. Since all have been born from relatives from Eve, we also inherit the sin she and Adam received. It is the reason as to why we all get sick and die. Question. Was the world of our ill-fated ancestors free from any accidents? Was it impossible to fall off a cliff? Was it beyond feasible that in the future it would have been impossible to be hit by a car? What does perfection mean? Did perfection extend to Gods created animals? I watched a stinkbug fall from a light onto my dining room table, it landed upside down and it could not right itself. I watched for a long time, looking to see what mechanism it would use to flip itself. Nothing. What a poor design from our Lord. Is this a flaw generated by the "Fall"?

Now there are those that have absolute faith in the creation myth although science has disproven the idea of an actual Adam and Eve. During the time that the so-called Adam and Eve procreated, there were already other humans on earth which supports evolution and disproves the Genesis creation account. Adam and Eve had brothers and sisters. It is just a fundamental fact that *their* offspring did *not* survive. However, this contradicts the Bible wholeheartedly. *"So God created mankind in his own image, in the image of God he created them; male and female he created them."* – Genesis 1:27

There are others who believe that the creation account is an allegory or a polemic. However, that would eliminate the biblical first couple, and without Adam and Eve, the entire bible collapses! Jesus is stated to be the second Adam. *So it is written: "The first man Adam became a living being"; the last Adam, a life-giving spirit.* – 1 Corinthians 15:45 How can there be a second Adam if the first Adam did not exist?

The most important consequence however in this concept of an allegorical Genesis account is that it is impossible for a literary construct to commit sin, so therefore sin would not have occurred, and original sin would not have permeated into all of the subsequent lives of human beings. Original sin is somewhat of an inherited trait. Just like we can acquire our straight or curly hair from our father and our eye color from our mother, original sin is a characteristic obtained by our original mother, Eve. We need to, however, understand original sin. What is original sin?

Original sin is the doctrine that states that since Eve and Adam (in that order) disobeyed Yahweh in their perfect state, they were made imperfect and therefore their successive children would inherit this imperfection.

"Therefore, just as sin entered the world through one man, and death through sin, and in this way death came to all people because all sinned.

It's As Original As Sin

To be sure, sin was in the world before the law was given, but sin is not charged against anyone's account where there is no law. Nevertheless, death reigned from the time of Adam to the time of Moses, even over those who did not sin by breaking a command, as did Adam, who is a pattern of the one to come." – Romans 5:12-14.

Since we are all children of Eve we have in biblical terms all been born imperfect and defective in the eyes of our Lord. We now need to serve God fully without recompense, dutifully serving him through our own accord and with minimal fault. Question. If the biblical King Solomon, who had direct access to God himself, was the richest person there was, so he didn't need to succumb to things because of money and was granted all of the wisdom in the world thereby making him the smartest man to have lived at that time; if he could not follow God properly, how does God expect us to do better?

First, this is highly unfair. Since when should the crimes of our parents have any bearing on our current standing? If an adult committed a crime should the sentence be also inflicted upon its entire lineage? How is that fair? Should we as humans be paying the penalty for our great-great grandmother's infractions? Should our scales of liberty be tipped with the insolence of previous transgressions?

There is a more menacing side to the doctrine of original sin, however. If we are born sick of this disease known as imperfection, then we need a cure. What is the remedy? Anton Chekhov once stated, *"If there's any illness for which people offer many remedies, you may be sure that a particular illness is incurable, I think."*

Doctors may provide cures to what ails us, but the Bible offers only one antidote. The sacrifice of a perfect human man. *"For since* death came through a man, the resurrection of the dead also comes through a man. For as in Adam all die, so in Christ, all will be made alive." – 1 Corinthians 15:21-22. The eternal one will balance the scales of justice by cleansing what Adam blemished because apparently a woman's life does not have any value in the bible. It was Eve who committed the first sin by eating the fruit from the tree of knowledge of good and evil. Eve was perfect when she "sinned" and therefore should have needed compensation when it came to the scales of justice. However, since women are rated at the scale of chattel, the human creators of the myth did not think about this conflict. "You shall not covet your neighbor's wife. You shall not set your desire on your neighbor's house or land, his male or female servant, his ox or donkey, or anything that belongs to your neighbor." – Deuteronomy 5:21. Notice how the woman is lumped into slaves, land, and oxen. Regardless of this fact, the original sin doctrine dictates that a perfect man, the son of God Jesus, was required as a permanent sacrifice for humankind insolence. However, is this moral?

A scapegoat is a person who is blamed for the crimes, mistakes, and wrongdoings of other people. In biblical times, the scapegoat was a being that received all of the sins from the tribe and was cast out into the wilderness, a way of extrication of one's sins. The first account of this occurrence in the Bible is in Leviticus. "He is to cast lots for the two goats--one lot for the LORD and the other for the scapegoat." – Leviticus 16:8 In other translations it is stated that "He is to cast sacred lots to determine which goat will be reserved as an offering to the LORD and which will carry the sins of the people to the wilderness of Azazel." Azazel means either fallen angel, absolute removal or scapegoat. It was a ritual in which the sins of the tribe were placed upon a goat, and this sin infested goat was removed from Israel and outcast to the desert during the Day of Atonement. It is this very concept that the Bible uses as a construct to absolve Adam and Eve's offspring from this so-called sin.

Jesus Christ was the perfect and final sacrifice that was offered to Yahweh, a perfect weight to balance the scales and make Jehovah pleased and satisfied. The problem is the morality of the sacrifice. If it is not moral and downright stupid to use an actual goat to heap the sins of a tribe upon, how does using a human sacrifice make any more sense? Why did Jesus have to *die* for the sins of humanity? Is not the more moral option for God to have just *forgiven* us instead?

Is death truly required for recompense to God? If so, please understand that God plays parlor tricks with the people. If he requires death as due compensation for humanities sins, then he is guilty of more than sleight of hand. When an animal sacrifice was presented as an imperfect sacrifice to God during the biblical times of Israel, the animal died. Its life was given to Yahweh. Now, when the ultimate sacrifice via God's only begotten son, he was raised three days later! What kind of sacrifice is this? What was so courageous in what Jesus accomplished? If this were the only means of salvation, any one of us would have sacrificed ourselves to God with the knowledge that we were going to be raised three days later. It would have been tantamount to partaking in a three-day nap! How is this a sacrifice? Would it be a sacrifice to lend a person $5,000.00 if it was guaranteed that you would receive the same $5,000.00 in three days? If not, then the sacrifice of Jesus should be viewed in the same manner. It was not much of a sacrifice at all!

Furthermore, what about the events that lead to the crucifixion of Jesus. *"When evening came, Jesus was reclining at the table with the Twelve. And while they were eating, he* said, "Truly I tell you, one of you will betray me." They were very sad and began to say to him one after the other, "Surely you don't mean me, Lord?" Jesus replied, "The one who has dipped his hand into the bowl with me will betray me. The Son of Man will go just as it is written about him. But woe to that man who betrays the Son of Man! It would be better for him if he were not born." Then Judas, the one who would betray him, said, "Surely you don't mean me, Rabbi?" Jesus answered, "You have said so." – Matthew 26:20-25

How does destiny play into this nefarious original sin doctrine? Since the Bible teaches the doctrine of destiny, was there ever a reality where Judas did not betray Jesus for 30 pieces of silver? Apparently not if everything is predetermined. Judas had no choice but to turn Jesus to the authorities. If he had no choice in the matter, why would Jesus expect anything else from the person who would betray him? Why punish Judas and say that it would be better for him if he were not born?

This then brings us to the garden of Eden, where this nonsense all commenced. Was there ever a universe where Eve did *not* eat from the fruit from the tree of the knowledge of good and evil? Did Eve ever have a choice as to what to do when the temptation by the Satan was proposed to her? If God is omniscient, then he knows all and therefore knew that Eve would have eaten the fruit all along! If that is the case, then Adam did not have a choice in the matter when it came to eating from the fruit that was provided by Eve. If you follow this line of reasoning, then you cannot blame the devil for what he did. Lucifer was *compelled* to taunt and tempt Eve with the forbidden fruit.

In the end, this all appears to be a game set into motion by the very creator who wanted subjects to worship him, provided the

It's As Original As Sin

illusion of free will but then let the movie of time play out its fanciful scenes in public. God then created a religion and engineered its operation to the public to ensure that everyone played their role, especially religions adherents. What religion does is create a mental panopticon, a liturgical construct that houses the mind of the parishioner that provides no refuge for thoughts that are contrary to pontificated doctrine. This is why you have individuals confessing their "sins" or separating themselves from the intellectual conversation when it conflicts with paradoxically inerrant belief. There is an embedded intrinsic fear of a supernatural being that is always watching you, hovering to each one of your destinations, inscribing an accurate account of the ebb and flows of your imperfect life's journey and your mission is to please him. The true horror lies in the supposed fact that if your deeds prove you to be unworthy, this spiritual phantasm has the power to effectively end your existence. The power of fear is debilitating, yet it provides a safe haven for the person under the restraint of faiths manacle. Resistance may occur during indoctrination, but it too is ephemeral. In essence, religion is the Pavlovian instrument used by Pastors to embed sinister mental machinations into our evolved soul.

It is becoming obvious that the religious doctrine of original sin, coupled with destiny was not created by an omniscient being. It was generated by an ancient animal sacrifice cult, the one found in the old testament and has human origins, not a divine one. What does this mean for Christianity as a whole? What are the consequences of this knowledge? It must be fundamentally clear that religion is not an enterprise that which people should base their lives on. However, is it too late to stop the growth of religion?

Chapter Nine

Luke: *Ben! Why didn't you tell me? You told me that Darth Vader betrayed and murdered my father.*

Obi-Wan: *Your father... was seduced by the Dark Side of the Force. He ceased to be the Jedi Anakin Skywalker and "became" Darth Vader. When that happened, the good man who was your father was destroyed. So, what I told you was true... from a certain point of view.*

Luke: *A certain point of view?*

Obi-Wan: *Luke, you're going to find that many of the truths we cling to depend greatly on our own point of view.*

A scene from Star Wars: A New Hope

The perception of the sacred biblical word can only be discerned in a certain light of a specific religion when you see it from the theological viewpoint of the religious observer. There is a danger in all of these stories where abhorrent tales are viewed as spiritually beneficial or teachable.

The Parasite That Will Not Die

So, where does this leave us in our struggle to understand the pervasiveness of religion? After every failure of religion, what explains its enduring metamorphosis and the plasticity of such fables that carry such great worth to generations and generations of past and current human civilizations? This acrimonious animosity between religion and reason may never be reconciled, regardless of how sanguine anyone may profess to be on the debate. The issue at heart here is twofold in that people of religion have valid humanistic reasons for feeling the need for a creator, and there are those who identify themselves with a particular religion that may not actually believe its basic tenets in the privacy of their own minds, but will, regardless of reasoning, display unwavering adulation over their religion's primacy. We must endure with an overwhelming majority of people who ingest their morals in scroll form and who worship a deity, who yearn its rewards and fears its wrath. Their lives are achromatous in nature, with no flavor other than savory religious bits that they hold dear. Their primary goal is to bow down to their parental dictator and to rely on it for everything, because as it is said in the Christian organization as a whole, *"do not be anxious about your life, what you will eat or what you will drink, nor about your body, what you will put on"* because God will provide everything you need. In addition to needing a savior, they have an aura of perpetual immunity to criticism of their chosen deity. No one can challenge the principles of their faith, without fear of a direct or indirect attack on their person. Others believe they have a god given right to murder other people who do not align with their understanding. Two examples are the Christians during the era of the Crusades and Islamism.

However, if we look at the two major subsets of religious groupings, weekend believers and fundamentalists, an imagined dividing line becomes apparent, and that vector is the path to mental sanity. That is not to say that this path is the correct path. The truth is always the best destination, a place where the heat of intelligence evaporates faith and where the flood of knowledge dissolves concentrated religious ignorance. However, to many, this unification of understanding may seem to be an unreachable panacea that this society can never sustain, so they shift their attention to more banal goals. Instead of focusing on goals with true substance, they search for that ontological bedrock where society lies and then use that as their foundation. Unfortunately, that bedrock is assumed to be constructed with nonquantifiable morality, an area where it is stated that science has no dominion over and religion once again takes hold upon its hovering perch and paralyzes the populace with its regurgitated teachings. This is clear parallelism to Mathew 16:18 which states *"Now I say to you that you are Peter (which means 'rock'), and upon this rock, I will build my church, and all the powers of hell will not conquer it.'* In the end, this cycle will continue ad infinitum, unless we act. More on that in the subsequent chapter. With religion always being allowed to enter the fold with a hedge to any logical questioning, one would have to be a simpleton to give up such a position. Once established, these very religious organizations will continue to smuggle in perverted moralistic shackles covertly disguised as the inherent tautology of codified doctrines. This handcuffing of current and new parishioners is essential for maintaining order within an entropic organization. It is these very shackles that create the chaos that envelopes various nations and divides many families and is the very reason why religion and science can never be reconciled.

This overlapping of magisteria between science and religion has no place in this society. Furthermore, the spheres of influence that religion holds should be exorcized immediately since corrective mechanisms do not truly exist in religion. Whereas science has experiment, peer review and public inquiry, in addition to advocating intellectual honesty and integrity, religion has faith and nothing more. Religious faith looks for truth that coincides with their beliefs like apologists. Apologists are nothing more than pseudo-scientific individuals looking for reconciliation. They have no interest in the truth and only care for the marriage between biblical accounts and ideas that consecrate this marriage.

Why is it that the creation account in Genesis does not convolve with scientific fact? Apologetic gymnasts will state that the account is written from the perspective of an earthly observer. An observer on the first day would have seen the diffused light from the newly formed sun slightly permeate the thick atmosphere of this early earth. It would take until the fourth day that the two great luminaries were discernable on earth and that is why the bible states that the sun and moon are created on the fourth day. Apologists would state that the account would need to be viewed from a certain point of view to reconcile what is written and fact. This harkens back to the previous dialogue found in Star Wars at the beginning of this chapter and is a constant element that they return to whenever needed.

This is why the parasite of religion will not die. Please understand why websites like Answers In Genesis and literature like the Jehovah's Witnesses Watchtower are written. The literature is a device for influencing one's understanding and not a device for providing true information. The questions that are asked are intended to generate a specific answer. If information is what is truly being requested, literature that is non-dogmatic, secular and scientific in form is the only vehicle.

The Parasite That Will Not Die

The only vehicle used by fundamentalists and apologists alike is fear. For Jehovah's Witnesses, if you decide to study via means of secular "propaganda," then God will judge you in the end. If you do not accept an apologist's answers that do not jive with reality, then you have been tainted by the world or "this system of things." Fear is a very powerful force that was discussed in a previous chapter. It is a motivator that can make the most rational person believe in nonsense.

Why is it when an accredited apologist generates stories that are so far fetched but reconcile the bible that they are believed, but if another person were to try they would be considered crazy? Here is my attempt to reconcile Christmas and Christianity. As Daniel (of Bible lore) once did for king Nebuchadnezzar, interpreting his troubling dreams, the following Danielian logic can be applied to the following Christmas interpretation.

Santa, the all-powerful being at the end of the year is God. The end of the year signifies completion of his test to humanity and the "new year's resolution" is the abnegation of humanities will and the installation of Gods will. God provides gifts to those who believe in him and his disciple's pronouncements and allows suffering to those who reject him. The army of Elves are his myriads of Angels, spiritual beings that assist God in his quest for his will. His floating sleigh is tantamount to Ezekiel's Wheel, the vehicle of God mentioned in the Bible book of Ezekiel. The reindeer are the cherubim of Ezekiel's Wheel, the propulsion of the vehicle, under the guidance of God. The harness Santa uses for the reindeer is the holy spirit that guides the cherubim in its direction and speed. It is also an allusion to how God directs humanity in its course. The milk and cookies allude to the offerings the Israelites gave to God as per the prescription of worship given to Gods people in the bible.

The Parasite That Will Not Die

It can also be compared to the charity work that religion often does and boasts about. Providing charitable work in exchange for everlasting life is a spurious reason for administering it. The Christmas tree is congruent to the tree of the knowledge of good and evil as mentioned at the second chapter of Genesis. Gifts of eternal life in heaven (or on earth, depending on your beliefs) are lavished upon the good people while reparations of coal, an allusion to heat/hell is administered to the rest of humanity.

If the belief of Santa is preposterous like my attempt at apologetics, then what do we call the belief in God? In the end, it is an extraordinary story that is propped up only by the scaffolding of faith. It is a legend that was passed down from generation to generation via oral tradition or mythological writ, handed down by our fearful predecessors. Our progenitors entrusted this instruction upon us, albeit false information, to help us weather the storm of reality. However, we as modern humans have assimilated these fables as fact, without any true empirical evidence as a foundation. The reality is that humans have built their entire culture upon an unsteady base, religion. The apostle Paul said it best in 1 Corinthians 3:11 – *"For no one can lay any foundation other than the one already laid, which is Jesus Christ."*

Even though these fictional stories should in no way guide the lives of humanity, unfortunately, this does not seem to be the case. Take 26-year-old Éloïse Dupuis for example. On October 12, 2016, Éloïse died, seven days after giving birth to a healthy baby, due to multiple organ failure. The only treatment that could have saved this woman's life was a simple blood transfusion. However, due to her faith in the Jehovah's Witnesses religion (another collection of Christian fables), she could not accept blood transfusions. It is because of the concretized faith of this person that she is dead.

Why is it that religion itself will not die? Well for one reason, current religion cannot be mocked in any manner, at least in this current political climate. We can joke incessantly about believers of Zeus, Odin, and Thoth but cannot be critical in the least bit about Yahweh, Allah or Jehovah. Why the parallelism between these deities? What common thread do they all share? They are all myths and yet, they, the current gods of our time, must be handled with white glove service while their criticizers are put out to pasture. The gods of Egypt, Mesopotamia or ancient Greece/Rome have no currency in this world because they are extinct, but any current major religions are absolved of any ridicule. Why is that?

Another reason for why the parasite known as religion will never perish is that there is no right way to conclude that you have wasted all this time believing in something that is wrong. Imagine if you spent ten years of your life to receive a Ph.D. in Ombiography. Your parents also spoke about this field your entire life and couldn't wait until you attended college to study this very discipline. After being immersed in this thinking, how would you feel when someone proved that Ombiography is not a true field of study? How difficult would it be to conclude that everything you were taught was a lie?

An additional reason can be the creation of sin, which exists nowhere except for religion. Sin is a transgression against divine law. Divine law can only be found in the sacred texts of religion. Religion can be a vehicle in which man-made sin can be blotted out of existence. In the Christians case, this occurs with the crucifixion of Jesus the Messiah. I can only compare the act of absolution of sin via a human sacrifice by gods son, or God himself, depending on which fabulist doctrine you ascribe to, with the book "The Whipping Boy" by Sid Fleischman, a book I read in school when I was about ten years old. The plot is quite familiar. The prince is a spoiled brat, hence is aptly named "Prince Brat." As a prince, he could never receive physical punishment for his actions, since he is royalty, so he is given a whipping boy who is beaten on every occasion that this Prince commits an infraction. It is humans that have become spoiled brats and Jesus who must bear the sins of all humanity. The premise of "The Whipping Boy" to the average person would be detestable, but it seems like morality is placed in the religious blind spot followers conveniently have when Jesus' sacrifice is mentioned.

One other reason can be the reinterpretation of religion and its fluid dynamic for quasi-believers. The apostle Paul declared that women are not permitted to teach. However, there are Christian churches that have women as ordained ministers. Homosexuals are now making excuses for God with regards to how they are portrayed in the bible. If you search online, you can now find gay-affirming churches. That is quite hard to swallow when you have verses in the bible such as the one listed below.

Because of this, God gave them over to shameful lusts. Even their women exchanged natural sexual relations for unnatural ones. In the same way, the men also abandoned natural relations with women and were inflamed with lust for one another. Men committed shameful acts with other men and received in themselves the due penalty for their error. Furthermore, just as they did not think it worthwhile to retain the knowledge of God, so God gave them over to a depraved mind so that they do what ought not to be done. They have become filled with every kind of wickedness, evil, greed, and depravity. They are full of envy, murder, strife,

deceit, and malice. They are gossips, slanderers, God-haters, insolent, arrogant and boastful; they invent ways of doing evil; they disobey their parents; they have no understanding, no fidelity, no love, no mercy. Although they know God's righteous decree that those who do such things deserve death, they not only continue to do these very things but also approve of those who practice them."
- Romans 1:26-32.

This scripture describes how gay people deserve death, but still, some homosexuals would like to be a part of a Christian church! That is tantamount to the Jews making a case for wanting to be a Nazi in Nazi Germany! If you feel that this statement is grossly overblown, please reread the scripture mentioned before and ponder on it. Incomprehension is the myopic lensing of true understanding. Apparently there is a fine line between obvious and oblivious.

There are those that will declare that the confusion and the veracity of religion is the very reason for religious debates. However, why is this topic up for debate? Why is math, science or medicine not up for debate? It has to do with the empirical evidence on the side of the aforementioned disciplines. Religion only has faith to prop itself upon. Apologists can contour any existing data to coincide with the divots in religions surface. The idea is tantamount to the concept of Maslow's hammer, popularly phrased as *"if all you have is a hammer, everything looks like a nail.'* If an apologist is armed with the Bible and faith, anything that can contort to their beliefs, no matter how flimsy the data, is viewed as a solution to their reconciliation issues.

In summation, the foundation created for religion is based on a lie. It is as if all of the Christian religions religious fundamentals were fashioned by the same 3D printer, fitting the impressionable mold of piety that is self-evident today. No amount of supplication to the heavens can create a partner to converse with. Talking to the wind will not provide a reply. Propitiations to a man in the sky will not be reciprocated. The immaterial gift of God is not bestowed upon you unless you believe in an imaginary entity in the heavens. It is by the continuous and eager hope for the potential but false apocalyptic conclusion that keeps humanity in the clutches of past legends. The is the very gestation of ideas and the incubation of its promulgations that allow the parasite of religion to enter our bodies, contaminate our souls and use our bodies as vessels for its procreation and dispersion, via public action, declaration or the most alarming of its mechanisms of dispensation, evangelism.

Furthermore, we have to deal with believers that only have a glancing acquaintance of their holy text, but a puritanical faith that is unshakable. Belief without evidence is a dangerous way to live. Unfortunately, this is where we find ourselves today, surrounded by religious authorities that use this very foundation to keep religion alive. What is the solution to the lies propagated by religion in this world?

Chapter Ten

"When we have to change an opinion about anyone, we charge heavily to his account the inconvenience he thereby causes us."
- Friedrich Nietzsche

We are unfortunately confined to the confabulations of past humans, their fears vulcanized into the codified doctrines of societies current religions. There have been many movements in history to excise these archaic concepts, but religion is like the criminal organization Hydra of Marvel comics fame. *"If a head is cut off, two more will take its place."* This saying actively describes the topographical landscape of religious belief and the aftershocks we are forced to endure. As previously mentioned, the fuel for the propulsion of these logically arcane but highly recognized and even welcomed ideas is faith.

Exfoliating The Blemished Fingerprint Of Humanity

Admonished by the Bible at 2 Corinthians 5:7, spiritualistic emotions impelled and stylized by mythology should be the driving force behind our actions. However, *if we walk by faith and not by sight*, we would immediately hit a tree, person, car or other object and we would inflict harm to ourselves or others. Impending death is certain. I understand that the aforementioned scripture is an ideological construct and should not be taken verbatim but to understand faith is to recognize that faith is always to be taken literally. When a person of faith says they believe in a God that made us and saw us from his perch above, this is exactly what they believe. When a person says to one that has lost a child in birth that "God needed another angel," this is precisely what they envision. When a person says "God has a plan for me", this person actually presumes that God has mapped out a path in life for them and had all of their needs; emotional, financial and spiritual, fully explicated in great detail and that these arrangements have been somehow transcribed in their destined future life map. If faith is to be correctly understood, then we must correctly discern that the aforementioned scripture can only be taken literally. However, there will be automatic pushback from society for this declaration, itself an inherently compressed spring of misguided understanding.

What does that mean for our struggle with religion in society? It indicates that humanity has unconsciously placed a security blanket on the mental shoulders of those seeking spiritual comprehension. Safe spaces have been carved out as havens for dogma to roost. It allows faith-based interlopers into an arena of conversations that they have no place in occupying and provides a proverbial trumpet blast to those who have no skill in playing the instrument of knowledge. The security blankets are the hijacking of certain terms, such as faith, hope, and belief. Their safe spaces are the confines of political correctness and the human's insistence for coddling.

If you question their beliefs, they provide caveats at every instance, as you have seen from the previous chapters. Why do they protect their religion? The commanding viewpoint is that without religion, society would crumble upon the weight of its own sin, sin being a suitcase term created by religion to keep us as subordinates under the manacle of religious leaders. They ask "If you remove religion, what do you replace religion with?" Using this same logic, if you remove a spousal abuser, what do you replace it with? The removal is what resolves the issue! There is no need for a replacement! However true this is, there may be things that religion partakes in that future secular organizations must take up the mantle and assume responsibility for. We will discuss this in more detail at the end of this chapter.

Another reason for the undying existence of religion? People in power want to stay in power. It is said best in this exchange in the movie "Pumping Iron."

Arnold's friend: *"The king of the hill can only go down, Arnold."*

Arnold Schwarzenegger: *"or stay up."*

Arnold's friend: *"Right. That's the other possibility. But the wolf on the hill is not as hungry as the one climbing the hill."*

Arnold Schwarzenegger: *"That's true, he's not as hungry. But when he wants the food, it's there."*

If you have reached the top of the mountain, metaphorically speaking, like a pinnacle position in your career, you would never want to genuflect to another individual and rescind your standing. If this is the case with the average person, why would we believe that men in power in Christianity would like to give it up? Why should we expect for persons in this level of hierarchy to do the right thing and dissolve the religion that has single-handedly committed the most atrocities in the world? If there is a God and he sees Christianity's instinct to commit crimes against humanity and to subjugate its adherents to a lifestyle of false piety, why has he not done anything about it?

Why would a God create a partisan religion that only certain people would cling to? Why would God create a religion period? Is it to be understood that God, the architect of the universe, the elementary particles and everything in between including all biological lifeforms, cares about our singular wellbeing? Whom of us has tried to sustain an ant farm? We can stare in amazement at how they interact with each other and how they move individually but do we care? I am a huge animal lover and even I, after watching for two weeks the tribe of ants move to and fro in the farm, am not personally afflicted by the sole death of every ant. Are we saying that God, the provider of all life and the creator of our infinite surroundings is capable and more so even cares about our feelings and wellbeing when you calculate the number of humans that have existed and died in the history of the earth? The bible says so but is it even possible? The bible says that we are all made in the image of God, but that does not mean that

Exfoliating The Blemished Fingerprint Of Humanity

we look like God, for God is massless and is not restricted to a form. Therefore we must surmise that the image that we were created in are certain qualities he has. Love, strength, and wisdom are a few that come to mind, and yet still he has created a religion that divides people in the billions. God only views people in tribes. He is not personable.

When a child or teen dies, a Christian may state that, *"he or she was too young to die, that parents are not supposed to bury their young."* However, that is always followed up with *"He is in a better place."* Does it really pass for knowledge to tell someone who has just lost their significant other or child that they are better off away from them, in the profundity of their misery? Is it even true? Is a child better off with or without their loving parent?

Religion may never die due to the supposed comfort that it brings. Prayer has been foisted upon parishioners as a way to directly communicate with God as a means of comfort. However, what has prayer ever done that was beneficial? If two football teams pray for victory, one of their prayers will not be fulfilled. The Islamic hijackers of United Airlines Flight 93 were praying to God before they attempted to hit their intended target. The ironic thing is that the passengers prayed to God as well. What good did any of their prayers do?

Religion also allows people to pose the questions of the *why* affirmation. Why do we exist? Why were we created? Why is there suffering in this world? Why did God take my son so early? A friend of mine once forcefully questioned; *"Why have you eliminated the possibility that there is a God and possibly one that actually cares about us?"* My response was

Exfoliating The Blemished Fingerprint Of Humanity

"That is the last question you should be asking yourself, the why." Imagine that your daughter just killed her newborn son. The first question you would ask is why? And rightly so. Your daughter is sentient and therefore could have decided to do that heinous act of her own accord. There is agency to her act. However, you would do better to ask the more immediate questions, who what where & how! So, your daughter killed her son. What happened? Where did it happen? How did she do it? After you gain all of this understanding, *then* you can ask them why. But what if the situation has to do with inanimate objects. What if a tree fell on your daughter's son and killed him? You can go through the four immediate questions (minus the who because this is an inanimate situation) and that will give you all of the answers you would need. But what if you asked why? The why is trying to attach agency to this situation when none exists. If you ask a religious person why this occurs, they would respond that it is because Man has sinned. Therefore sin infected the earth, and because of that, bad things happen. The state of the earth is ripe with decay, and in some instances, trees fall on people. God will fix this matter shortly though. However, this thought is *assuming* that there was agency in this event. Assuming such can actually force an answer, and not provide a correct one. How about space, another place full of inanimate situations? The religious or generally inquisitive person may ask, why did the universe come to be? Why are we here? The issue is the same as seen previously in inanimate situations, the why is diametrically opposed to the other four more pertinent questions. You can see that in the people who ask the questions. Scientists ask

Exfoliating The Blemished Fingerprint Of Humanity

"What made the earth exist? Where did this occur? When did the process start? How did it happen?" The religious side of questioning. Why did it happen? You can see that the question divides people into two groups — the ones who want answers in the actual and the ones who want to answer such a question philosophically. It does not necessarily make the why question wrong to ask but remember what I stated earlier. The why question is the *last* question you should ask if needed. Once you know *all* of the pertinent information that was gleaned by scientists, *then* you will be in a situation to decide if a why question makes sense. Was agency actually *needed* in order for the universe to occur? You can always ask why but don't always expect an accurate answer.

Why did I go through this long and tedious diatribe about the question why? The answer lies in the original premise. Religion allows people to pose questions of the *why* affirmation. If the why question is the least important question to ask, then religion, which is based on the why principle, is the least important discipline on earth.

If religion is the least important field of understanding but is responsible for so much harm, why do we allow it to exist? It is similar to having an argumentative relationship with a close family member. You know how to resolve the issue, but since the topic is so sensitive and requires great effort, the person is content with keeping the status quo. We all know there are steps that we can all take to abolish religion, but since that would require the broaching of so many sensitive topics, we have been content with the way things are. We need to step out of comfort zones and plant a flag for all to see with regards to the goal we should all have and that is the dissolution of religion. There is a good deal of steps so although the list may sound ominous; they are by no means insurmountable.

Step 1 in removing religion from its position of power would be to revoke all tax exemptions on religious establishments. The wheels of this step have already been set into motion with the lawsuit by the Freedom From Religion Foundation which targets the "parsonage allowance" which is, in essence, a housing allowance for pastors and other religious employees. I will not go into specifics and the history of the church's tax exempt status with the IRS. However, we should all be aware that *everyone*, even people who are not religious and are even atheists are indirectly subsidizing religions by means of their paying of taxes. If we were to remove this tax exemption, churches would need to become self-sustaining to survive and not rely on government handouts. This removal would devastate many churches and lead them to close down.

Step 2 would be to make it criminal to teach an idea that is proven truly false. How many times have we been frustrated and angered when we hear that children have been physically abused? We all would like to free that child from the confinement of those bad parents or guardians. Why are we not just as angered when we hear that these children are being taught that the earth is flat? Where is the condemnation when told that these kids are being taught that the Holocaust never occurred or that the NASA never landed on the moon? We should be just as alarmed by these allegations. Why? Imagine what these false ideas and concepts do to the growth of an individual? Imagine what else is being taught by a Holocaust denier. Imagine the stunting of scientific understanding a child would go through if they were taught that the earth was created in 7 days or 10,000 years. Imagine a world where these concepts and other outlandish ideas are believed by the majority of society! What type of world would we be living in?

Holocaust denial should be criminal. Lies spread about the civil rights movement should be illegal. Anything that we can definitively provide as accurate and true should be against the law to teach. Now, I am not condoning the use of the government to infiltrate our kitchen tables and living rooms to see if these ideas are being taught at home. I am merely stating that if these concepts are being taught in public or it can be determined that these false teachings are being learned in private, that there should be a penalty paid for this abuse. This would include the false teachings taught under the guise of the bible. The earth was not created in 7 days. The sun did not stand still during the battle against the Amorites. Seizures are not the effect of demonic possession. All of these teachings and more can be demonstrated to be false. We, as decent human beings should not tolerate this abuse to our children and others who are taught these falsely arcane concepts. These thoughts and ideas are absurdities and as Voltaire once stated, *"those who can make you believe absurdities can make you commit atrocities."*

Step 3 in the process of the abrogation of religion would be to change the word "theory" to "fact." The term "theory" has been hijacked by religion to mean that a concept is merely a hypothesis and stands on shaky ground. The reality is that a theory is the most established idea in all of science! However, since the religious reality is that a theory is not a fact, plentiful arguments can be made against many established certainties. According to almost any Abrahamic faith, the theory of evolution is just that, a theory, something that cannot be proven true. The fact of the matter is that the evidence on evolution is greater than the evidence on gravity. So why is it easier to absorb gravity than evolution? Because we can experience gravity? We may be able to experience firsthand the effects of gravity, but the fossil record gives us undeniable and overwhelming proof that the theory of evolution is true, more so than gravity. In addition to the fossil evidence, we have DNA evidence that we evolved from earlier primates. We also have visual cues that current primates are our cousins. Our ears, eyes, skeletal organization and even our fingernails and fingerprints indicate a close relationship with our primate ancestors.

The reality is that the evolution of the word "belief" is comprised of the residue of false past ideas, including one that a theory is merely an educated guess. I, therefore, declare that we should replace the word "theory" with "fact" so that we would call our coming into existence the fact of evolution. If you wanted to describe the beginning of the existence of the cosmos, you would reference the "Big Bang Fact." Einstein's greatest achievement would be considered the general and special fact of relativity. This simple change would eliminate the confusion that people have when the word theory is used.

Step 4 in this process is to teach religion in schools as mythology. The current religions are often beatified as the true paths towards understanding. We need to be mindful that in the past many other religions were in this position of power and have now been relegated to the cluttered graveyard of past religions. The only difference is that the religions that people hold dear are contemporary. Not long ago the Roman gods were worshiped. The gods of ancient Egypt once had the same reverence as Yahweh, Allah or Jehovah. Thor and Zeus were once prominent gods. Greeks used to pray to them for intercession in their daily lives. What is common in all of these religions is that they are now taught as mythology in schools. Why should any of the contemporary religions be any different? Its only reason for existence is the public belief in these false ideas. In many respects, religion is like The NeverEnding Story. In the novel/movie the fantasy world Fantasia can only exist if you believe in it. If you stop believing, Fantasia and religion will fade from existence and can only be read about. Religion is an attempted substitute for intelligence and wisdom. It is, however, a poor attempt. God is not real.

Step 5 in the removal of religion is by teaching critical thinking at the High School level. Critical thinking is the ability to assess given or perceived information in an objective manner to make a reasoned conclusion. Currently, High Schools teach information required to pass tests via rote memorization. The power to decipher situations or ideas and make reasoned judgments is not a skill that is taught to high schoolers. It's important for students in High School to learn these tactics since it would assure that people who forgo a college education can have this armamentarium in their arsenal for everyday life and especially when religious discussions take place.

Step 6 is that the language that is currently used must be changed. The only way religious thoughts can be evacuated is if the OS of the human mind is upgraded. That OS is Language. We need to utilize our wetware properly. Language has inherent biases, and this is the gimmick that religion uses to keep people in line. Take a table of balls for example. If there are a large number of balls on the table and we ask them to describe the quantity with language, we would get many responses. A lot of balls. A ton of balls. Plenty of balls. However, if you were forced to describe the quantity of the balls with numbers only, everyone would say 212. No one would say 1000 or 50 or 1. The language that you use greatly affects people's answers to questions and also their ideas, concepts, and beliefs.

To explain why we need to change our language game when trying to eradicate religion, let's take people for example. Many times the question has been asked: "If you could be someone else, who would you be?" The problem with this question is that it is not possible to become someone else and not because of technological reasons. A persons very being are its sentience being exposed to certain conditions or memories. These conditions that make us who we are and shape us are recorded as synapses in our brain. These pathways, under most circumstances, are permanent unless another condition overrides them. Who we are is not our "life force," for lack of a better phrase. If we were able to transfer our life force to another person, since our very being is made up of a pattern of synapses, the person who receives this life force would perceive nothing. Nothing would change, and we would not be that new person.

Exfoliating The Blemished Fingerprint Of Humanity

We would have lost our lives for nothing. It is similar to a river. The river water shapes the river bed through erosion. The water may create new channels for the water to flow through over the years and a "traumatic event" like a flood could severely alter the river bead. If you were to remove the water from the river, the river bed remains and the locations of its tributaries, streams and all. If you were to replace the water you would not change the river in any way. It would continue to flow as it did before. The river bed is our brain. Unless exposed to new experiences (minus age and illnesses) our brains will not change.

Society is very similar. The societal landscape has been carved out from past experiences and has provided itself as a suitable host for the parasite known as religion, due to its exposure to it. Certain words have been created and hijacked from standard vernacular to mean something else. These words have made religious people Manchurian Candidates of sorts in that they now react to these words and act according to their faith. These "religious" words or phrases need to be excised from our vocabulary so that society can change and be made a less habitable host for religion. Just like hieroglyphics were useful for the Egyptians but not for the Romans, we need to evolve our language with the changing times and out of necessity. Roman numerals were replaced by Arabic numbers because of the invention of zero and the place system that allowed calculations to be made easier. Newton created the language of calculus to intellectually express the laws of physics. When we hit the limits of a language, we need to modify it in order to become less socially biased.

We now need to abolish faith-based language, so that trivial argument like *"is there a God"* will no longer occur since illogical arguments will no longer be able to be expressed. We should in earnest modify our current language to emancipate illogical thinking and statements. There are some words that should be removed from our vocabulary. Those words which are faith, belief, imperfection, and sin should be expunged from our contemporary terminology — these terms illicit illogical reasoning, which is primarily responsible for religion. It is like politics. Those who are not fully aware and informed of the issues have no business discussing them. Encouraging people to speak logically will allow for healthy discussion to permeate our society.

Step 7 is to have secular charities take over the roles once assumed by religious churches. We must realize that many charitable causes are fulfilled by the churches of the United States. If religion would cease to exist, many soup kitchens and homeless shelters would be shuttered. However, we need to understand that giving to others to please your god, because he has commanded that you give to the poor, is not a good reason for giving! We should want to give to others in need from the bottom of our hearts. Everyone should donate what they can every month to a non-religious entity (even if one has a religious past) such as Goodwill, Doctors Without Borders, UNICEF and Amnesty International. We should also donate *directly* with people in need so that 100% of the proceeds go directly to the person or family in need. Furthermore, to truly be effectively altruistic, we should all try to open charities that are focused in the town we live in. This will maximize the wellbeing and reduction of suffering in your town and should bring great joy to your heart.

The 8th and final step is to allow time to heal the wounds religion has inflicted by allowing societal evolution to remove these faith-based tendencies and leanings. It is my optimistic confidence that I get to see religion lose its tightening grasp on humanity during my existence, but that would involve such a great change in society in such a short period of time. It is my expectation that my children's children would see the fruits of this labor if these changes were placed into effect today. I urge that you take these steps with great determination and fearlessness. I also ask that you teach these steps to others as well. The changes will not work until the majority of the public follows these measures. Please remember that although important to the cause, the true solution is not the un-indoctrinating of a person because then there will always be others that fall into religion. The resolution is to stop a person from being infected with the parasite known as religion in the first place.

Can we abolish religion? Is it even possible? Take the civil rights movement from the '50s and '60s. Racism permeated the air. There were segregated seating areas for black people. Black individuals could not even *drink* from the same drinking fountains as whites. However, blacks persevered, and now racism has been greatly reduced. Things that would be considered appalling to the majority of whites then, are now commonplace, and this is all due to the steps African Americans took to make themselves equal, as stated in the United States Declaration of Independence. Please remember that such obvious forms of racist behaviors are only approximately 70 years old. Look at what can be done in such a short period of time.

In times past women were separated in college. There were men only courses. Women were not allowed to vote and were treated as second-class citizens. Now, women makes up approximately 47% of the workforce in the US. There are still biases inherent in society with regards to women, but it is because of the steps they took during the women's rights movement that allowed them to progress so far in society. The days of women being treated as lesser human beings is over. Why can't we hope the same for religion? When will the Humanist Rights Movement begin?

Does this mean that we need to remove all aspects of religion in order to emancipate ourselves from its shackles? Absolutely not! This is not to say that we need to abscond the majority of traditions generated by religious organizations. To omit from our lives the religious holidays and any other established practices would be throwing the baby out with the bathwater. There is no need to have life denuded of all sacred embellishments to create utopia. I personally love Christmas regardless of the religious entanglement this pagan holiday contains. The staunchly religious aspects of the tradition I avoid, such as the depictions of Jesus in the manger surrounded by three wise men or the idea that this is the birthdate of Jesus. As long as religious lies are not pontificated, I see no problem. However, conclusions like circumcisions would be avoided at all costs. Circumcisions only occur due to the Judeo-Christian

Exfoliating The Blemished Fingerprint Of Humanity

God's requirement upon the Israelites to circumcise as a symbol of Gods covenant with his chosen people.

Nonetheless, since God does not exist, why would anyone foist such barbarism when it only occurs because of adherence to the current worlds norms. As the late and great Christopher Hitchens once said *"Handed a small baby for the first time, is it your first reaction to think, "Beautiful, almost perfect, now, please hand me the sharp stone for its genitalia that I may do the work of the Lord"?* See how religious creep can compel us to do things that we would not normally do? If we can avoid the religious aspects of a tradition, regardless of the amount of circumlocution one may undertake, holidays are not an aspect of religion that needs to go by the wayside.

Regardless of our view on religion, there is no need to provide a 'tear the band-aid quickly' attitude towards its abolition. Each step should be done methodically with the expectation that at the end of the line we will live in a society in which false mythology has no currency in.

What is a religion? Religions are stories generated by humans about humankind which state why we are special and why we are not animals. The antidote, regardless of its depressing tone, is to realize that we *are all* animals and nothing more. Please give mindful consideration to this. Give a person the Bible with no further opinions, leanings or spin, and they will find cruelty in the vast majority of the text. This is the fingerprint of the writings of man, not of God. In the end, we should not look for our destiny in dusty old texts. The late and great Carl Sagan said it best. *"We're made of star stuff. We are a way for the cosmos to know itself."* Never should we allow ourselves to be controlled by this parasitic infection. Feed it the antidote of knowledge and critical thinking. The heavens do not contain a God. We should find our consolations in the constellations.

Chapter 1: The Religious Reality

Andrews, Evans. History.com. 2013. 8 Reasons It Wasn't Easy Being ▸artan. Web. https://www.history.com/news/8-reasons-it-wasnt-easy-ing-spartan

Starr, Bernard. Huffingtonpost.com. 2013. Why Christians Were enied Access to Their Bible for 1,000 Years. Web. tps://www.huffingtonpost.com/bernard-starr/why-christians-were-nied-access-to-their-bible-for-1000-years_b_3303545.html

Livio, Mario. Huffingtonpost.com. 2017. Who Predicted the cistence of the Planet Neptune? Web. tps://www.huffingtonpost.com/mario-livio/who-predicted-the-isten_b_3719234.html

Squires, Nick. Telegraph.co.uk. 2009. Pope Benedict XVI: condoms ake Aids crisis worse. Web. tps://www.telegraph.co.uk/news/worldnews/europe/vaticancityandhol ee/5005357/Pope-Benedict-XVI-condoms-make-Aids-crisis-worse.html

McConnell, Anna. Agriculture.com. 2018. An Overview of Irrigation echniques & Technology. Web. tps://www.agriculture.com/machinery/irrigation-equipment/an-rerview-of-irrigation-techniques-technology

Chapter 2: Fear Brings About Religion

Kushnir, Yochanan. Columbia.edu. 2000. Atmospheric Forces, Balances, and Weather Systems. Web. https://eesc.columbia.edu/courses/ees/climate/lectures/atm_dyn.html

Schmarzo, Bill. Dell EMC. 2013. Understanding Type I and Type II Errors. Web. https://infocus.dellemc.com/william_schmarzo/understanding-type-i-and-type-ii-errors/

Ripley, Francis. Catholic.com. 1993. Transubstantiation for Beginners. Web. https://www.catholic.com/magazine/print-edition/transubstantiation-for-beginners

Chapter 3: Religion Finds A Host

Chalakoski, Martin. Thevintagenews.com. 2017. Many Icelanders believe that the Huldufólk, a race of elves, live among them but in smaller houses. Web. https://www.thevintagenews.com/2017/12/15/huldufolk-iceland/

Mingren, Wu. Ancient-origins.net. 2016. Huldufolk: Supernatural Creatures Hiding in Iceland. Web. https://www.ancient-origins.net/myths-legends/huldufolk-supernatural-creatures-hiding-iceland-005870

Roberts, Oral. Inspiration.org. 2009. 3 Keys to the Seed Faith Principle. Web. https://inspiration.org/christian-articles/seed-faith-principle/

Chapter 4: The Parasite Begins To Feast

Mayo Clinic. 2017. Tapeworm infection. Web. https://www.mayoclinic.org/diseases-conditions/tapeworm/symptoms-causes/syc-20378174

Jemison, Micaela. Smithsonian. 2014. Crazy eyes and mind control – the power of parasites. Web. https://insider.si.edu/2014/11/crazy-eyes-mind-control-power-parasites/

Heschel, Susannah. The Aryan Jesus. 2010. Princeton University Press. Book.

Brown, Derren. Netflix.com. 2018. The Push. Web. https://www.netflix.com/title/80220000

Chapter 5: Logic As Medicine - Morality

Nordqvist, Christian. Medicalnewstoday.com. 2018. What to know about antibiotics. Web. https://www.medicalnewstoday.com/articles/10278.php

Basics, Vaccine. Vaccines.gov. 2017. Vaccine Basics. Web. https://www.vaccines.gov/basics/index.html

Brom, Robert. Catholic.com. 2017. Mary: Mother of God. Web. https://www.catholic.com/tract/mary-mother-of-god

Chapter 6: Science As Medicine - Facts

Sirven, Joseph. Epilepsy.com. 2014. What is Epilepsy? Web. https://www.epilepsy.com/learn/about-epilepsy-basics/what-epilepsy

Choi, Charles. Space.com. 2012. Exploding Star May Have Sparked Formation of Our Solar System. Web. https://www.space.com/16943-supernova-explosion-solar-system-formation.html

Pariona, Amber. Worldatlas.com. 2018. Timeline Of Mass Extinction Events On Earth. Web. https://www.worldatlas.com/articles/the-timeline-of-the-mass-extinction-events-on-earth.html

Natural History Museum. 2018. Birds: The Late Evolution of Dinosaurs. Web. https://nhm.org/site/research-collections/dinosaur-institute/dinosaurs/birds-late-evolution-dinosaurs

Rao, Joe. Space.com. 2018. Solar Eclipses: When Is the Next One? Web. https://www.space.com/15584-solar-eclipses.html

Teasers, Brain. Relativelyinteresting.com. 2018. The Bat and A Ball Problem. Web. http://www.relativelyinteresting.com/the-bat-and-a-ball-problem/

Chapter 7: The Problem With Belief

Sunderland, Terry. Forest News. 2011. Killed for keratin? The unnecessary extinction of the rhinoceros. Web. https://forestsnews.cifor.org/4876/killed-for-keratin-the-unnecessary-extinction-of-the-rhinoceros?fnl=en

Loder, Vanessa. Forbes.com. 2015. Can Stress Kill You? Research Says Only If You Believe It Can. Web. https://www.forbes.com/sites/vanessaloder/2015/06/03/can-stress-kill-you-research-says-only-if-you-believe-it-can/#79706891682e

Jenkins, Aric. Fourtune.com. 2017. Which Is Safer: Airplanes or Cars? Web. http://fortune.com/2017/07/20/are-airplanes-safer-than-cars/

Nace, Trevor. Forbes.com. 2018. Flat Earther's Genius New Idea: We Live In A Magical Pac-Man World. Web. https://www.forbes.com/sites/trevornace/2018/05/02/flat-earthers-genius-new-idea-we-live-in-a-magical-pac-man-world/#6a8d1d581e5f

Mathewson, Samantha. Space.com. 2018. Ant Nebula Blasts Lasers, Suggesting Hidden Double-Star System. Web. https://www.space.com/40648-ant-nebula-blasts-lasers-double-star.html

Chapter 8: Its Original As Sin

Burton, Neel. Psychologytoday.com. 2013. The Psychology of Scapegoating. Web. https://www.psychologytoday.com/us/blog/hide-and-seek/201312/the-psychology-scapegoating

Chapter 9: The Parasite That Will Not Die

Fleischman, Sid. The Whipping Boy. 2003. Book.

References & Citations

Chapter 10: Exfoliated The Blemished Fingerprint Of Humanity

Reily, Peter. Forbes.com. 2018. Appeals Filed On Ruling That Exemption Of Clergy Housing Allowances Is Unconstitutional. Web. https://www.forbes.com/sites/peterjreilly/2018/02/16/appeals-filed-on-ruling-that-exemption-of-clergy-housing-allowances-is-unconstitutional/#6520cd17487a

Made in the USA
Monee, IL
29 June 2020